HOW TO DRESS A
NAKED
PORTFOLIO

A TAILORED INTRODUCTION TO
INVESTING FOR WOMEN

BEVERLY J BOWERS

**How to Dress a Naked Portfolio: A Tailored Introduction
to Investing for Women**
Published by Sister Courage Publishing
Chandler, AZ

ISBN: 978-0-578-31270-5
BUSINESS & ECONOMICS / Personal Finance / General

Cover and Interior design by Victoria Wolf, wolfdesignandmarketing.com.
Copyright owned by Beverly J Bowers.

This primer is dedicated to my grandchildren—Maiya, Madilynn, Damon, Lucia, Nova, and Kian—and my partner's grandchildren—Elliott and Elinor.
I love you to the moon and back!

CONTENTS

INTRODUCTION

AS THE DAUGHTER OF A MUSIC/MATH TEACHER in the Midwest, I grew up loving both subjects; but had little exposure to the world of business, except as a consumer. Education was a priority in our home, as you can imagine, and I entered college focused on a traditional female occupation following in the footsteps of my older sisters. It only took a few months to know that it was not the right fit for me. I longed for a way to apply my love of math, and that led me to economics. I endured the base-level courses and eventually fell in love with classes on money and banking. I wanted to be a banker!

My introduction to the world of banking came when I was offered a job in the investments area of the trust department of a Midwestern bank. With patient teachers, I learned the basics of stocks and bonds and how they trade, and I was forever hooked.

That was many years ago and, while much has changed, much has not changed in the world of finance and investments. It is still a male-dominated industry but with a growing female presence and strong female role models. In one way or another, it has been my passion to encourage women, both in the profession and as investors. I find it especially rewarding to help women who are starting to invest—to dispel the mystery and simplify the process.

However, as an investment advisor, wealth manager, and financial planner, my client meetings were typically attended by men, and they were the ones who made the financial decisions. Sometimes a female spouse/partner was not interested in being involved, or it was inconvenient for her to do so. However, I believe that often it was a lack of understanding, and in some cases, real intimidation that kept her away.

Equally troubling to me has been the scarcity of ways for a beginning investor to gain knowledge. Fortunately, the financial industry and its regulators recognize there is a gap and are making efforts to address it. Until those resources are widely available, how can beginners learn? Those with substantial assets may choose to hire an advisor. However, that option is not available or desired by everyone. If a person has access to an employer-sponsored company retirement plan, the company or the plan representatives may help employees understand the basics. However, those who do not have that option are often left to learn on their own.

How to Dress a Naked Portfolio is a primer for beginners: women interested in investing who have no prior experience and women who want a basic understanding of the investment process. How can I introduce financial concepts to women who have no prior exposure? I have chosen to compare saving and investing to shopping and selecting an outfit—shoes, clothes, and accessories—because it is a process familiar to most women. The content will cover saving and investing basics and define related terms. Review questions at the end of each chapter highlight key points, and definitions of italicized words or phrases appear in the Glossary.

I chose the topics included in this step-by-step guide. My intent is to provide the essential information necessary to encourage you to begin to invest, to help you understand the process, to generate confidence, to spark further interest . . . and to have fun doing it! Once you begin, I am sure that questions will arise. Please feel free to share your comments and questions with me on my website. I will address the most frequently asked questions in my blogs. I would also love to hear about your investing progress, so keep me posted.

If you desire personal investment advice or wish to know about insurance-related products, please seek an appropriately licensed advisor who is a **fiduciary**, a person who holds a legal and ethical responsibility to put your interests first.

Thank you, and happy reading!

Bev Bowers

bevbowers.com

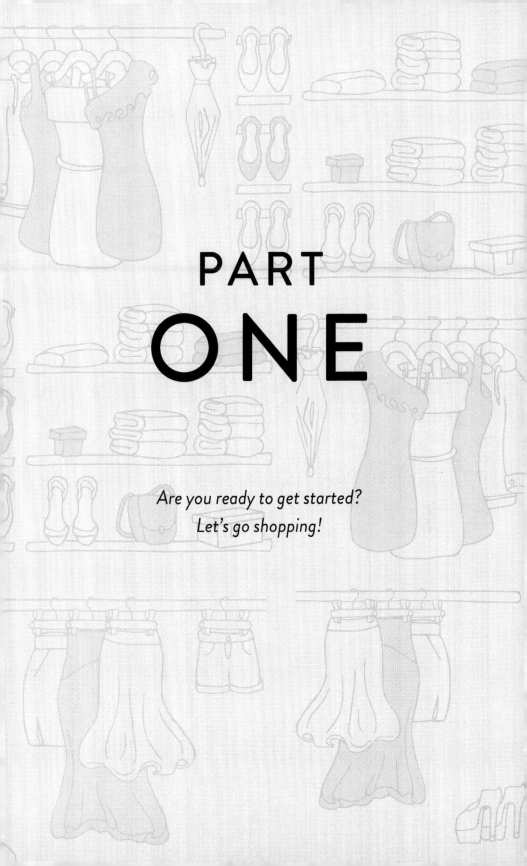

PART
ONE

Are you ready to get started?
Let's go shopping!

CHAPTER ONE:

SHOPPING

MOST OF US DO NOT WANT TO WASTE MONEY, but that is easier said than done. After a spring cleaning of my closet, I recently went shopping for a pair of jeans. I found the jeans, but...I also found a cute top, only to bring it home and discover that, oops, I have another top almost like it hanging in my closet. No wonder I liked it! Ever done that? We are less likely to make costly mistakes if we give shopping more thought. Of course, I could return the new top, but that takes time, and, more likely, it will hang in my closet and not get much use.

If I were smart, before I went shopping, I would take a quick inventory of my closet and think about what I really need. NEED, now that's a concept that seems to go by the wayside when I shop. I know that I NEED jeans, but do I really NEED another top, or is that a WANT? Do you know the difference between NEEDS and WANTS? The fashion magazines and retail stores are good at converting WANTS to NEEDS, so how good are you at resisting impulses? Sometimes yes and sometimes no? Hey, we are human. What will stretch my clothing allowance further, though, is a decision to resist buying anything but jeans. I will fulfill my NEED but not my WANT.

What kind of jeans should I buy? Do I follow the latest fashion trend or a more classic style? Do I prefer Western or designer jeans, leggings, crops, boot-cut, or straight line? Lots of choices. For me, that is an easy decision, and I bet it is for you. You know what makes you feel good and is also comfortable, even if your preference changes over time or with the season. So, if I want to resist buying anything else, and I need that pair of jeans, where do I shop? From all the choices out there, what store will likely have what I'm looking for—a department store, a specialty retail store, a vintage shop, a consignment shop, or an online store?

Also playing into that decision is my *budget*. (There is a sample budget at the end of the chapter.) How much can I spend? This is either an easy question to answer or a hard one. First, it assumes that I have a budget and have allocated a certain amount of money to clothing purchases and know how much I can afford to spend. If I have done my homework, I know what the pair of jeans I need will cost, or at least a ballpark number. I don't want to pay too much, and I want to recognize a bargain. Who doesn't love a bargain? Finally, are there any extra expenses, such as sales tax or shipping fees, which will add to the cost? In my case, I had room in my budget and an idea of the cost of the jeans.

Now I know what I need to buy and how much I can afford to spend and have an idea where I can find it. I am ready to buy. For me, that means heading to the mall, as I love to shop where I can try on jeans for the best fit in a couple of stores. Should I take a friend or go it alone? Maybe some of you want and can afford to have someone shop for you. I prefer to shop for clothes alone, so out the door I go.

EIGHT SHOPPING QUESTIONS

- Why am I shopping?

- What will it cost?

- What is my style?

- Where can I find it?

- What do I already have?

- What are my choices?

- Are there other expenses?

- Do I want help?

These eight questions apply to investing as well as to shopping. We will go step by step through each one of them. There are basic terms that will help you select your investment outfit, and we will discuss those. Please do not allow yourself to be intimidated. A little time spent up front will make your decisions so much easier. You can do this!

By reading this primer, I assume that you have some interest in investing or at least want to understand the process. How in-depth you want to go is up to you. Investing can take as much time as you want to give it. The decision is yours. Do you want to build your portfolio piece by piece, or do you want a quick and easy solution—one and done—or somewhere in between? Do you prefer to learn on your own? Do you want to take classes, or do you want to pay an investment advisor to make *investment* decisions for you? Lots to think about.

REVIEW

1. What is the difference between a NEED and a WANT?

2. What are the eight shopping questions?

The exhibit that follows is a sample budget. Please become familiar with it. You will learn more about it and use it in review exercises in later chapters.

EXHIBIT – SAMPLE BUDGET

	January	February	March
INCOME			
Wages/Salary			
Spouse/Partner Wage/Salary			
Pensions/Social Security			
Dividends/Interest			
Other			
TOTAL INCOME			
EXPENSES – FIXED			
HOME			
Mortgage/Rent			
Electric/Gas/Water/Sewer			
TV/Phone/Internet			
INSURANCE			
Health			
Home/Rental			
Auto			
DEBT			
Car Payment			
Credit Cards			
SAVING/INVESTING			

EXPENSES – VARIABLE			
FOOD/HOME			
Groceries			
House/Cleaning Products			
TRANSPORTATION			
Fuel			
Repair/Maintenance			
License			
MEDICAL			
Doctors			
Prescriptions			
PERSONAL			
Clothes/Shoes			
Hair/Nails			
DONATIONS/GIFTS			
TOTAL EXPENSES			
INCOME (MINUS) EXPENSES			

CHAPTER TWO:

WHY AM I SHOPPING?

TO MAKE A SUCCESSFUL SHOPPING TRIP, you need to know your reason(s) for shopping. I need jeans, for example. When it comes to saving and investing, the answer could be any of these: your employer offers a 401(k) or other *company retirement savings plan*, you inherited some money, you want to save for a big purchase like a car, or maybe you just sold your home. You might be saving for your vacation next year, for college in five years, for your retirement in thirty years, to help your children, to support causes you love, or to provide for your family after you die. Maybe it's because you are interested in the stock market and how it works. There are lots of reasons, and each one can be called a financial goal.

Financial goals are spending, saving, and investing targets you hope to achieve over a set period. They vary with lifestyle and stage of life. If you are young, you may save for a special dress or your first car. Those are shorter-term goals. When you start a family, your goal may be to own a home or put money aside for your child's education, and it is never too early to plan for retirement. Those are longer-term goals. You may have education debts to pay, which could be either a short-term or a long-term goal. Setting financial goals is critical.

Goal setting is not a one-time event. It is an ongoing process. For example, when you enter the workforce, your goals might include buying furniture for your apartment, travel, and hopefully, starting to invest for your retirement. You meet someone special and decide to become a couple. Your goals now include another person, and together, you set new priorities. Children may enter the picture, and once again, your goals change. There is, however, one goal that lasts your whole life, and that is eventual retirement. Please give priority to investing for the kind of life you want when you retire, and along the way, celebrate as you meet your goals.

You might find the following six financial goal-setting steps helpful:[1]

1. Figure out what matters to you. What do you value? (Freedom from debt, charitable giving, your or a child's education, etc.)

2. Sort out what is within reach.

3. Apply a SMART-goal strategy. Are your goals Specific, Measurable, Achievable, Relevant, and Timely?

4. Create a realistic budget. (See previous chapter exhibit.)

5. Automatically transfer any leftover funds to an account to address the first couple of things (priorities) on your list.

6. Monitor your progress.

Spend time making a list of your goals. If you are like most people, you have multiple reasons to save and invest. Does it then make sense that funds for each goal, or group of goals, might be invested differently? Do you wear the same outfit to the beach that you wear out to dinner at a classy restaurant? Of course not. What separates your goals?

We will separate goals based on two factors: time or *time horizon* (how long before I need the money?) and *liquidity* (how easily can I turn my investment into cash?).

HOW LONG BEFORE I NEED THE MONEY?

A rule of thumb says that funds invested in the stock market should be kept in place for a **minimum** of five to seven years. Why is that? Because the stock market moves around every day, even throughout the day, and sometimes prices go up and sometimes down. To give the market time to recover from any downturn and maximize the potential for growth, you'll want to leave the funds invested for a period of years. Because *volatility*, the movement of prices up and down in the market, has increased over the years, the longer you can stay invested, the better.

However, **and this is important**, if your goal is short term, then do NOT invest that money in the stock market. If you do, you may find that when you need the funds, you can't sell your stocks without taking a loss. That possibility exists.

To separate the difference between short term and long term for this primer, we will use five years as the dividing line. Short-term investing (less than five years) will be called SAVING, and long-term investing (five years or longer) will be called INVESTING. Got it? In this primer, your *portfolio*, your completed outfit, will consist of your choices of ways to save and your choices of ways to invest.

HOW EASILY CAN I TURN MY INVESTMENT INTO CASH?

The second question to ask yourself is, "Once I reach my time goal, how quickly will I need to convert my savings or investment to cash?" Do you need all the money right away, or will the need be spread over a period? You may have a firm date. For example, I will do my Christmas shopping right after Thanksgiving, or I will take my vacation next August. Maybe college or tech school is a few years off. The start date is an easy date to determine but remember that your expenses will be spread over several years. The beginning of retirement may be a harder date to estimate, but more likely than not, it will be more than five years away. Right? Again, the need for funds in retirement will be spread over many years, a much longer period than education. Take your list of reasons you want to save and invest and group them into short term and long term using five years as the dividing point. A template is provided in the chapter review.

HIGHEST PRIORITY GOAL: AN EMERGENCY FUND

What is an *emergency fund*? It is money set aside for the unknown surprise. Rules of thumb say that it is good to keep between three to six months of your base expenses separate to cover any unexpected situations, such as the COVID-19 pandemic. Recent experience suggests that six months of base expenses may not be enough, but what you choose to set aside for emergencies depends on your comfort level. Your emergency fund should be easily accessible and liquid.

What is a base expense? Base expenses are sometimes called *fixed or non-discretionary expenses*. They MUST be paid every month: mortgage/rent, utilities (electricity, gas, water, sewer), communication (TV, internet, phone), car loan or other loans, etc. Do you have a list? If not, make a list now of the expenses you MUST cover each month. Then, although they are variable from month to month, add an average of what you typically spend for groceries and transportation. Also include those items unique to you and your household, such as prescription and medical expenses, which recur and are essential. Do not include the cost of clothing, eating out, or travel for vacations, which are referred to as *variable discretionary expenses*. They are not essential. The sample budget template at the end of Chapter One will be helpful.

NOTE OF CAUTION

Combining funds meant for saving (short-term goals) with funds primarily meant for investing (long-term goals) increases the possibility that you might confuse their purpose. My recommendation is to keep them separate. How do you do that? Well, there are stores that specialize in *securities* for saving, and there are stores that specialize in securities for investing. Think of it this way: REI carries sports clothes, as does Lululemon, while Kohl's and Target carry a selection of clothes for work, dress, or sports. They all carry clothes for sports, but some also offer clothes for a broader variety of occasions.

The reasons for saving and investing are unique to you. No one is the same age with the same lifestyle, income, expenses, family circumstances, and tastes as you. Your priorities will be different. Your priorities are also likely to change over time, so it is important to revisit this exercise periodically, no less than every five years or when you have an important life-changing event: marriage, birth, death, or divorce, for example. Especially in the world of investing, it is tempting to compare notes with a friend or family member. I urge you to honor your unique needs and save and invest accordingly.

REVIEW

1. Using the budget template from Chapter One and the instructions in this chapter, estimate how much to keep in your emergency fund. Include fixed expenses and an average of the variable expenses described. (Include only those items and amounts that are truly essential for living. For example, in an emergency, you may need to temporarily suspend TV service or your contributions to savings and investments.)

2. What are your reasons for saving and investing? Make a list of your goals and when you will need the money. Use five years as the dividing line between short term and long term. Example:

GOAL	WHEN NEEDED	LONG TERM	SHORT TERM
Emergency Fund	As soon as possible		X
Holiday Shopping	November		X
College	5 years	X	
Seminar	January		X
Wedding	10 years	X	
Retirement	35 years	X	

3. Why is it a good idea to keep your saving and investing clothes separate?

CHAPTER THREE:

WHAT WILL
IT COST?

WHAT WILL IT COST? Good question. How will you know if you can reach your goal unless you know how much you will need? Maybe you just prefer to save and invest when you can and then adjust your plans for spending, education, and lifestyle based on what you save. Does that really make sense? Do you expect to buy the designer shoes you love when your budget is more in line with a discount store? If you want a vacation to Europe with your girlfriends next summer, would you be able to pay for it with $500 from your savings? Not knowing how much you need is a huge risk and leaves the chance that, ultimately, you will not have the kind of life that you desire.

PAY YOURSELF FIRST

I've always loved this saying: "Pay yourself first." It means that you need to make sure you save and invest to cover your goals and needs **before** you buy other discretionary, nonessential (want) items. This may all seem so overwhelming, and the temptation is to do nothing. STOP!

How can you do it all? Maybe you can't, and that is okay. Prioritize your goals. If you have other important people in your life, talk with them to prioritize together. Work on the highest-ranked goal first.

A note to parents: It will be tempting to put the education of your children first, and that is commendable. However, remember that no loans or financial aid will be available to fund your retirement. I firmly believe that investing for retirement must be given a high priority.

> When oxygen masks drop in a plane, adults are instructed to put their masks on first, then their kids' masks. It's the same with saving for retirement.

CHANGING GOALS

What if your goals change over the course of your life? That is almost guaranteed. Marriage, divorce, children, death, or a serious illness will all affect your goals. I am told that between 80–90% of women will be solely responsible for their own or their family's finances at some point in their lives. Yet more than one in five working Americans doesn't set aside any of their income for either short-term or long-term goals.[2] In fact, a 2018 Federal Reserve study showed that more than 25% of Americans have zero retirement savings. To make matters worse, on average, each household with a credit card carries $8,000 in credit card debt, which creates an even bigger need for saving and investing.[3] It is time to reverse those troubling trends.

ESTIMATE COSTS

So, where can you find out how much your goals will cost? Here are suggestions:

- **Christmas:** See what you have spent in the past and increase/decrease as your gift list changes. Don't forget to increase for *inflation*, the likelihood that prices for the same items increase from year to year.

- **Vacation:** Check lodging, travel, food, and entertainment costs along the way and at your destination. Add them all up.

- **College/Trade School:** Visit websites of your favorite higher education choices or websites such as **savingforcollege.com** or **bankrate.com,** where you will input such things as your age or the ages of your children, whether you will attend a community college or in-state or out-of-state private or public college, and how much of the cost you intend to cover.

- **Retirement:** Many different calculators are available to help you figure this out. Choose a free one, such as **financialcalculator.org, smartasset.com, dinkytown.net,** or **finra.org**. Among the variables you will enter are your current age, starting age for retirement, current annual income, and current savings.

Many financial websites contain calculators. Compare results from a couple but beware of sites that use their calculators to promote and sell products.

COMPARE INVESTING PATTERNS

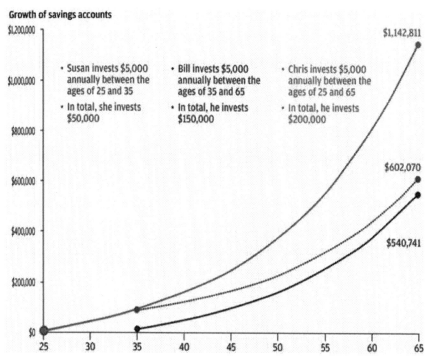

Growth of savings accounts

- Susan invests $5,000 annually between the ages of 25 and 35
- In total, she invests $50,000

- Bill invests $5,000 annually between the ages of 35 and 65
- In total, he invests $150,000

- Chris invests $5,000 annually between the ages of 25 and 65
- In total, he invests $200,000

$1,142,811

$602,070

$540,741

Source: J.P. Morgan Asset Management, *Guide to Retirement: Retirement Insights.* The above example is for illustrative purposes only and not indicative of any investment. Account values assume a 7% annual return.

The amount you choose to invest will depend on your resources and goals. As the chart demonstrates, it is better to start early and invest regularly. Even if you must stop after a few years, the *compounding* effect (additional income earned on both principal and reinvested income) can make a huge difference. In the world of saving and investing, what is *income*? It includes *interest* payments, *dividends* (profit distributions to owners or *shareholders*), and *capital gains* (profits from security sales) from your investments. Harnessing the power of compounding can greatly impact your result over the long term.

But what do you do if you are midlife and have not started to invest for retirement? It is time for a reality check unless you want to work at least part-time far into the future and/or have a drastically different lifestyle in retirement. Start by reassessing what you're spending. Look at your budget. If you do not have one, now is the time to create one. What spending can you cut to make your retirement a priority? How much can you invest every paycheck? If your employer offers a way to save for retirement, start there. Sometimes employers will even match what you set aside for retirement up to a certain percent. Take advantage of that. Is it possible to increase your income? Perhaps you could add a part-time job and religiously set aside that income for retirement. How about taking more risk with your investments? Although a slightly more aggressive stance (greater percentage of stock) may be appropriate, that carries with it the potential for increased volatility—bigger swings up and down in value. If that makes you nervous, you might panic and sell when the market is down and lose money. Before you make any drastic changes to your investments, think it through, and perhaps seek the help of a professional financial advisor who is a fiduciary.

COMMON INVESTING STRATEGY

A certain investment strategy may be helpful as you start. It is called *dollar cost averaging*. Using this strategy, an investor makes regular purchases of a specific dollar amount of a stock or *mutual fund* over a period. For example, after your initial investment, you decide to purchase $500 of a Total Stock Market mutual fund every quarter. The number of *shares*, or units of ownership, that $500 will buy will likely be different every quarter as the price of the mutual fund goes up and down. Sometimes the price will be high, and sometimes it will be low. Over time, however, the average price will be somewhere in the middle. Some mutual funds will allow you to set up for periodic investments on an automatic basis. This strategy reduces *volatility risk*, which is the risk of price swings not in your favor. It also eliminates the temptation to try to *time the market*, predict when the price will be at its lowest for a purchase or at its highest for a sale.

Dollar cost averaging is a great strategy for those with limited amounts of money to invest at any one time. When I graduated from college and started my professional life, I did not have an appropriate business wardrobe, nor could I afford to buy lots of clothes. I chose to make an initial investment in a couple of key pieces: pants and a matching jacket. Then, over time, I added a matching skirt and different tops and shoes and handbags to complement what I already owned. By putting aside money regularly to make those purchases, I gradually built my wardrobe.

No matter your age, it is rarely too late to start investing. As the graph in this chapter shows, it is better to start early so that the power of compounding can work for you. However, if you have over five years until the money is needed, investing is appropriate.

Please understand that there is no guarantee that your return will be positive, but the longer you remain invested, the better the chance of a positive return.

REVIEW

1. Take your goal chart from Chapter Two and assign a priority to each goal. I believe an emergency fund and then retirement and education should be the highest priorities; however, you may assign whatever priorities you choose.

2. Use your estimates, or one of the calculators referred to in this chapter, to come up with an approximate cost.

Goal	When Needed	Long Term	Short Term	Priority	Approx. Cost
Retirement	35 years	X		2	$1,350,000*
Holiday Shopping	November		X	4	$1,000
College	5 years	X		3	$125,000**
Seminar	January		X	5	$100
Wedding	10 years	X		6	$20,300***
Emergency Fund	ASAP		X	1	3–6 mos. expenses

*Estimate used the following inputs: current age 30; retirement age 65; current annual income $30,000; income increases 2% per year; no savings currently; desired retirement income is 90% of pre-retirement income; 30 years in retirement. Program assumes growth at 7% pre-retirement, 4% in retirement, 2.9% inflation, **and no Social Security. Source: https://www.dinkytown.net/java/retirement-nest-egg-calculator.html**

Estimated cost of a 4-year in-state public college in 2025. **Source: https://www.savingforcollege.com/calculators/college-savings-calculator

*****Source:** Hurst, Andrew. Average Cost of a Wedding: By State and Feature. Retrieved from **https://www.valuepenguin.com/average-cost-of-wedding**. (Not adjusted for inflation.)

Please do NOT let this scare you. It is a starting point but underscores the need to start saving and investing as soon as possible. Review the graph included in this chapter and note the positive outcome of regular investing.

3. How much can you save or invest quarterly? Divide that number by the number of paychecks in a quarter to get the amount to set aside from each paycheck.

4. Describe dollar cost averaging. Why does this strategy make sense for beginning investors?

CHAPTER FOUR:

WHAT IS MY STYLE?

THIS INVESTMENT QUESTION is not as difficult as it may seem. When you go shopping for clothes, handbags, or shoes, you are drawn to certain styles. You know that a certain brand of clothes–Ann Taylor, Old Navy, Levi's, etc.–appeals to your taste, and you may even know what size fits perfectly. If you are honest with yourself, you also know how careful you are with your money. Does money fly out of your wallet, or do you hold on tight? If you think about it, those characteristics may also carry over to other aspects of your life. Right?

If that is true, it will likely be the same with saving and investing. Let's say you like to take risks. How much risk is too much, and how much is not enough? When it comes to investing, various resources can help you determine your *risk profile* or *risk tolerance*. **It is the most important investment question to answer**. The right risk tolerance increases the likelihood that you will reach your investment goals. If you take on too much risk, your return might be greater, but you may get scared and panic and sell when the market is down. On the other hand, if you are too conservative, you may have to work longer or change your lifestyle to offset the lower return. Risk and return are related.

WHAT IS THE RIGHT AMOUNT OF RISK?

Most investing store websites contain a *risk tolerance questionnaire* or *risk assessment tool*. Why is it important? Because you want your investments to grow, but you don't want to worry day and night about your portfolio. The assessment of how comfortable you are with risk will help determine how much of your money should be invested in stock (riskier) and how much in *bonds* (less risky) and cash. A risk assessment tool or questionnaire provides a starting point for a basic investment outfit. An example of an investment risk tolerance assessment can be found at The University of Missouri Personal Financial Planning website: pfp. missouri.edu.[4] This assessment ranks your risk tolerance but does not suggest a particular asset allocation.

When you change the mix of the three *asset classes*—stock, bonds, and cash—the overall risk of your portfolio changes. The mix of the three is called *asset allocation*. According to the U.S. Securities Exchange Commission, "Many investment websites offer free online questionnaires to help you assess your risk tolerance. Some of the websites will even estimate asset allocations based on responses to the questionnaires. While the suggested asset allocations may be a **useful starting point** (author's emphasis), keep in mind that the results may be biased towards financial products or services sold by companies or individuals sponsoring the websites."[5] More about asset allocation later.

CONSIDERATION FOR COUPLES

It is often the case that spouses/partners have different risk tolerance profiles. Does one of you tend to push the boundaries and the other hold back and take a more conservative approach? How does that affect how you invest? What should you do? Start by comparing the results of your risk assessments and then discuss the differences. Is the difference a pattern in your relationship? If so, then this is no surprise. Is there a reason one of you feels more comfortable with risk? Perhaps you need to make up for lost time to reach a goal. Or maybe one of you grew up in a household that had to stretch to make ends meet, and the other was used to spending. A book that I have found helpful for couples who desire to understand and talk about their different money choices is *The Money Code* by Joe John Duran. It is an easy read and is available on Amazon.

If the difference between you and your partner is not major—one risk assessment suggests 60% in stock and the other 70%, for example—you may agree to start with the more aggressive allocation (greater percentage in stock). If the volatility is uncomfortable after a while, say a year, then reduce the amount of stock. If the difference in your risk assessments is major, 60% stock and 100% stock, you may decide to split your investments into multiple buckets and invest some more aggressively (greater percentage in stock) and some more conservatively (less invested in stock) to make you both comfortable. After your discussion, you may find a good compromise between the two risk profiles. There is no right answer. This may be a tough decision, but it is important to make your investments work for both of you.

HOW MUCH RISK CAN YOU AFFORD TO TAKE?

This question is equally important, and this is sometimes called your *risk capacity*. You may have a high tolerance for risk, but because of your personal circumstances, your capacity for risk is low—you can't afford to take undue risk. For example, imagine that you are mid-career, are the single source of income for your household, have two children in their teens, and have a small emergency fund but little saved for retirement or your children's education. Because of your family circumstances, your capacity for risk does not match your risk tolerance. Capacity for risk is affected by age, income, goals, and the time left to reach those goals. Your risk capacity may also be affected, but in a positive way, by the possibility of future financial resources: an inheritance, a trust of which you are a beneficiary, or a pension.

There may be times in your life when your capacity to withstand losses may be reduced. For example, if you are in an accident and need money to cover medical expenses, which require you to use your emergency funds and savings. Your financial resources, and perhaps even your income, are diminished. It may be appropriate to put a temporary stop to additions to your long-term investments until you are back on your feet financially. In any case, your emergency funds should be replenished before additions to your long-term investments. If the circumstances are severe and long-lasting, this may be one of the times that you also need to reassess your risk tolerance (your willingness to take risk) because of your reduced capacity to withstand losses.

Investing for the long term should only be undertaken when you have enough income and financial resources to cover your living expenses, have debt under control, and have set aside an emergency fund. After a review of your cash flow—income and expenses, debt, current savings, etc.—do you have enough left to invest? If you have the financial resources to invest, then you might ask, "Will I be able to save enough at current market returns to meet my long-term goals?"

The graph in Chapter Three demonstrates various scenarios for investing with a 7% return. If current market interest rates are near 7%, you may achieve a return of 7% with little risk. However, if current rates are closer to 1%, then it would take a significant risk to achieve a return of 7%. You can get an idea of the rate of return necessary to meet your long-term goals with one of the following calculators: **financialcalculator.org, dinkytown. net, savingforcollege.com,** or **finra.org**. Did you set a retirement investment goal in the review exercise after Chapter Three? If so, input that number in one of the calculators, as well as the number of years until retirement, the amount you currently have set aside for retirement, and how much and how frequently you plan to add to your retirement investments. Then vary the return to see what is required to reach your dollar goal. If you can't reach your goal with your current plan, or the rate of return necessary is not reasonable in current markets, then it may be necessary to adjust your goals or spending priorities. For example, you may have to delay retirement, take on a second job, put off education, or cancel your vacation plans.

Because investing involves risk, it is very important to properly assess your limits. Investing should only be undertaken after your basic needs are met, debt is under control, and funds are set aside for emergencies. For many of you, the first opportunity to invest will arise at work. Your employer may offer a way for you to set aside some of your pay for retirement. Because those funds will typically be invested for the long term, it is essential to understand your personal risk tolerance. When you shop, you rule out certain styles because they are just not "you." Your best friend may wear leggings when you prefer jeans. That is the same with investing.

REVIEW

1. Describe risk tolerance.

2. Describe risk capacity.

3. How are risk tolerance and risk capacity different?

4. If you have access to a computer, go to Vanguard's investor website: **investor.vanguard.com**. Using the search icon, type "Model Portfolio Allocation" and click on one of the choices with that name. Now look at the Historical Risk/ Return of the mixes of stocks and bonds displayed on the right side of the screen. Find the one that you feel matches your tolerance for risk. Especially focus on the Worst Year. How much downside would, or could, you tolerate?

   When you have decided on the best match for you, look at the left-hand side of the screen and note the mix of stock and bonds. What percentage of stocks and what percentage of bonds is suggested?

PART
TWO

With an understanding of the difference between needs and wants, you are armed to be a diligent shopper. You know your needs, your goals, and the approximate cost of each. You separated your goals into short term for saving and long term for investing and identified your investing style—your risk tolerance. It's time to hit the stores and pick out some clothes.

CHAPTER FIVE:

WHERE CAN I FIND IT?

BEFORE YOU START SHOPPING, it is important to differentiate between the places to shop—stores. Stores that offer clothes for saving are *banks, thrift institutions, and credit unions.* They might be compared to a specialty clothing store such as Victoria's Secret or Lane Bryant. Stores for investing are *brokerage firms* and *investment companies,* which are more like department stores. Some are lower cost, like Walmart or Ross or even Goodwill, and some are high end, like Saks Fifth Avenue or Neiman Marcus.

Do you like to shop at lots of places, or do you prefer to save your energy and shop only at a couple of your favorites? How will you choose when it comes to saving? Investing? Let's take a closer look at your choices of stores for saving and then stores for investing.

STORES FOR SAVING: BANKS, CREDIT UNIONS, AND THRIFTS

The main difference between a *commercial bank* and a credit union is that a bank is a for-profit financial institution, while a credit union is a cooperative and usually nonprofit. Thrifts are also for-profit.

COMMERCIAL BANKS

Commercial banks may be owned privately, by a family, for instance, or may be owned by shareholders (investors) and have stock that is publicly traded. Banks are focused on providing a return or profit to the owners or shareholders. They will typically have many locations for customer convenience and offer a wide variety of products/clothes and services. Clothes for saving will be described later. Some banks do not have brick-and-mortar locations but operate with an online presence, like Boston Proper, a women's clothing e-shop. You would expect online banks to have lower expenses because they do not have physical branches along with the associated costs. The savings might mean greater profit to the owners and/or better deals for customers, or a combination.

CREDIT UNIONS

Credit unions are owned by the people who use their services, their depositors or members, and return profits to their members in a couple of ways. Credit unions might pay a higher *rate of interest* (percentage you will earn) than a bank for money you deposit with them. Credit unions might charge a lower rate of interest (your cost to borrow money) for a loan than those charged by banks. The total interest paid to you on a deposit or that you pay for a loan depends on the *principal* (the dollar amount of the deposit or loan), the interest rate, the interest payment frequency (how often interest is paid or due: monthly, quarterly, or annually, for example), and the length of time over which the money is deposited or borrowed.

THRIFT INSTITUTIONS

Thrift institutions are *savings and loans and mutual savings banks*. They can be organized like a bank (owned by investor shareholders) or a credit union (owned by the depositors), but they are always for-profit. Thrifts offer many of the same products/clothes as banks, but traditionally, they emphasize consumer lending more than commercial or business lending.

STORES FOR INVESTING: BROKERAGE FIRMS AND INVESTMENT COMPANIES

When your living expenses are covered, your debt is under control, and you have built an emergency fund, it may be time to consider long-term investing. Two types of stores specialize in investment clothes: brokerage firms and investment companies.

BROKERAGE FIRMS

The store with the widest selection of investment clothes is a *broker-dealer, or brokerage firm,* a company in the business of buying and selling investment products (all kinds of clothes). A broker-dealer may be a person, a company, or another organization. They may sell their own clothes, and then they are called a *dealer*; they may sell clothes from outside sources, and then they are called a *broker*. Some investment clothes can only be purchased or sold through a broker-dealer because membership on an *exchange* is required, which is costly, like a private golf club.

The largest U.S. broker-dealer firms ranked by total *assets under management* in 2021 are Fidelity Investments, Charles Schwab, TD Ameritrade (its acquisition by Schwab was completed in 2020), and Edward Jones.[6] Are those names you recognize? They are not the only players in the broker-dealer world, however.

Independent broker-dealer firms were created for financial advisors who hold securities licenses but want support for a limited number of services, such as compliance and trade execution. Independents usually allow brokers more freedom in how they do business. If a broker has a strong client base that generates enough steady income to cover marketing and overhead expenses, then this business model might be attractive to the broker.

The largest independent broker-dealer in the U.S. is LPL Financial. According to *InvestmentNews*, the next six ranked by 2020 revenue are Ameriprise Financial Services, Raymond James Financial Services, Commonwealth Financial Network, Northwestern Mutual Investment Services, MML Investors Services, and Cambridge Investment Research.[7] These names may not be as familiar but think of them as retail clothing stores, not affiliated with a chain, that sell investment clothes manufactured by others.

INVESTMENT COMPANIES

A totally different type of store for investing is an *investment company*. Several types of investment companies exist, but for a basic portfolio, the applicable one creates *open-end mutual funds*, which are another type of clothes for your investment outfit. An investment company typically creates a wide variety of mutual funds (clothes), but some specialize in certain types of investments–stocks or bonds, for example–like Nike or Old Navy specialize in specific types of clothes. The store is the investment company, and the clothes are the mutual funds created by the company.

You can usually buy mutual funds directly from the creator store but not always. Some mutual funds are only offered via a brokerage store, and as you can imagine, the brokerage store may add extra fees. Therefore, buying a mutual fund directly from an investment company is kind of like buying wholesale, while buying via a brokerage firm is more like buying retail.

The largest domestic (U.S.) investment companies creating mutual funds, ranked by assets under management as of April 27, 2021, are BlackRock Funds, Vanguard Group, Charles Schwab, Fidelity Investments, State Street Global Advisors, PIMCO/Allianz, J.P. Morgan Asset Management, Capital Group Companies, and BNY Mellon (Dreyfus).[8] Heard of any of them? Some may be familiar because they have related broker-dealer stores. Some may be less familiar. PIMCO is best known for its bond mutual funds, for example.

You could complete an entire investment outfit–clothes, shoes, and accessories–from one investment company/mutual fund store. Think of it as purchasing an entire outfit from one designer or one brand. Sooner or later, you will probably want more diversity, however. Even for a basic investment outfit, choices are good. **The easiest way to buy mutual funds from many, many different investment companies is via a broker-dealer store.**

CAN SAVING AND INVESTING STORES BE RELATED?

Sometimes clothing stores are related: Chico's, Soma, and White House Black Market, for example. They cater to different clients and/or meet different needs but are brands of one company, Chico's FAS. Investing stores can also be related. You will note that some of the broker-dealers listed earlier are also on the list of investment companies creating mutual funds. Both are investing stores. The two functions, however, must be kept separate. They have different requirements, rules, and regulations.

Owners of stores for saving and investing can also be related; for example, Bank of America (a bank store) and Merrill (a broker-dealer store). Bank of America and Merrill are separate entities or subsidiaries of the same corporation. Again, the functions must be kept separate and have different requirements, rules, and regulations.

One cautionary word about shopping and stores. When you go to a store to shop for a new pair of jeans, what else do you see? Stores are good at placing items to entice you to buy what you do not NEED. That is one of the goals of marketing: to try to convert a WANT into a NEED. Remember the difference between NEEDS and WANTS? Some financial stores may also try to get you to buy financial clothes you do not need. That is called cross-selling, it is common, and it is not bad unless you allow it to control your choices. The more you understand yourself and can answer the questions raised in this primer, the more focused you can be on the type of clothes that you truly NEED.

Just as with clothes shopping, there are many choices for both saving and investing stores. Almost all have an online presence, but some may not have an office near you. If face-to-face interaction is important to you, consider those with offices nearby. Some will offer products/clothes or services not available at others. The larger companies will typically have a wider selection of clothes but may not offer the personal level of service that you desire. How do you prefer to shop? Think about it and keep reading. Additional tips are coming.

REVIEW

1. In which type of stores would you find savings clothes?

2. What is the major difference between commercial banks and credit unions?

3. What are the advantages of a commercial bank? Of a credit union?

4. In which type of stores would you find investing clothes?

5. Which investing store has more investing options (clothes) from which to choose?

6. What makes an independent broker-dealer unique?

CHAPTER SIX:

WHAT DO I
ALREADY HAVE?

IT IS CRITICAL TO KNOW WHAT CLOTHES you already have before you add more. What good is it to own five tops and no pants or skirts? Or to have purses and accessories but no shoes? To successfully put together an investment outfit, start by taking inventory. Your inventory should include the clothes you own in any saving or investing accounts. We will call the accounts **closets,** and the items they hold are **clothes**.

CLOSETS

In the world of saving and investing, you do not take the product/clothes home. Instead, you receive a receipt or confirmation of your purchase, but the clothes are kept at the store. You own the clothes, but the store is holding them in safekeeping; the store is the *custodian*. So how do stores keep your clothes separate from your best friend's, or your neighbor's, or your grandmother's? The clothes may be owned by people who live in another state or even another country.

HOW DO STORES KNOW WHICH CLOTHES ARE MINE?

When you buy saving or investing clothes, you open an account, which tells the store exactly who owns the clothes you are purchasing. The clothes and accessories you buy are then put into your account. We will refer to your account as a **closet**. The account title describes the owners of the items in the closet. Those owners may be an individual, a business, or two or more people together. They can even be a legal entity such as a *trust* or an *estate*. In addition to describing the owners, the name of the closet may tell the purpose for the clothes in the closet; for example, an *Individual Retirement Account* (IRA). The name of that closet says that the owner is an individual, one person, and the clothes will be used for funding retirement. Closets are sometimes called *ownership categories* or account *registrations*. Part Four of this primer contains a list of the most common types of closets.

Although you can't take saving and investing clothes home with you, you will go home with a receipt that describes your purchase and then receive periodic statements that list the clothes you own. The statement lists not only your purchases but also any sales or maturities, plus each item's *market value* (its current price, sometimes estimated). Statements are typically issued monthly or quarterly. You might be able to access your closets online as well. Online, the updates will be more frequent, often daily, or even during the day.

IF I CAN'T TAKE MY CLOTHES HOME, HOW DO I KNOW THEY ARE SAFE?

Most saving and investing stores offer some type of insurance protection for your purchases in case the store becomes insolvent—the unlikely event that the store is not able to return clothes to closet owners. Think of insurance protection as a money-back guarantee (up to a maximum dollar amount). The amount of insurance protection is related to the type of store in which clothes were purchased, and it is also related to the closet owner.

BANKS AND THRIFTS

The *Federal Deposit Insurance Corporation* (FDIC) insures deposits at commercial banks and thrift institutions. Insurance is offered according to the *ownership category* and how the accounts/closets are titled. The standard deposit insurance coverage limit is **$250,000 per depositor**, per FDIC-insured bank, per ownership category.[9] If you are a single person and have a checking account, a savings account, and a certificate of deposit at your favorite bank with a combined value of $300,000, only $250,000 will be covered by insurance. All of it would be covered by FDIC insurance if you moved $100,000 to a different bank or thrift store.

CREDIT UNIONS

Credit unions are covered by a different type of insurance – *National Credit Union Share Insurance Fund* (NCUSIF). The coverage is like that of the FDIC, and coverage limits are the same.

BROKERAGE FIRMS

Brokerage firms are covered by a federal insurance program, the *Securities Investor Protection Corporation* (SIPC). SIPC coverage provides up to $500,000 in **total** coverage (up to $250,000 of that for cash) per customer for lost or missing *assets*, cash and/or securities, from a customer's accounts/closets held at the institution. It also protects in case of unauthorized trading or theft from the *brokerage account*/closet. SIPC's coverage is based on *ownership capacities*, which are like ownership categories. Imagine you own two Roth IRAs at the same brokerage firm. For SIPC insurance purposes, they would be combined and together qualify for up to $500,000 of insurance. However, a Roth and a Traditional IRA would each qualify for up to $500,000 of insurance coverage under SIPC coverage because they are different types of closets. Note that SIPC insurance does not protect an investor from losses due to downward movement in markets.

INVESTMENT COMPANIES

Mutual fund assets are protected by regulatory controls set forth in the Investment Company Act of 1940. The act requires each investment/mutual fund company to place its mutual fund assets, cash, and securities with a qualified custodian, typically a U.S. bank. A custodian, as previously noted, is a company that holds assets in safekeeping.

HOW MANY CLOSETS SHOULD I HAVE?

In how many places should you save and invest? Of course, you can own closets at many different places, but if you have too many places, your time will be spent keeping track of the closets instead of focusing on the clothes within them. In other words, too many places may be counterproductive. How much time do you want to spend cleaning closets instead of shopping for clothes?

That said, you may need multiple closets just to meet your investing needs. You might have a closet in your name only, one in joint names (you and your spouse/partner), one focused on saving for retirement, a trust account/closet, and an account/closet for your business. If you are investing for college or tech school, you might have a 529 *College Savings Plan Account*. If your employer offers a company retirement savings plan, that account/closet will be separate. A list of common closets can be found in Part Four.

WHERE SHOULD I LOOK FOR EXISTING CLOSETS?

Do you already own some investments? Have you already started saving? Perhaps your parents or grandparents started putting aside money for your education. Maybe you will inherit some investments. Ask your parents, grandparents, or other relatives if they started saving or investing for you, and if so, ask if you could have a copy of the latest statement. (Sometimes money and financial topics are touchy subjects in families, so be sensitive to that possibility. If you can't get the information, assume you are starting from scratch.)

If you are married or have a partner, gather statements for closets you own together. If you intend to invest holistically as a couple (all closets, joint and individual, are considered together as one large walk-in closet), then also gather statements from your spouse/partner. Why do you need all of this information? You are taking inventory of your existing clothes before you go shopping for more.

As you collect and review statements, note what is in each account/closet. The items in a closet are clothes. Bank or credit union statements, for example, may list checking accounts, money market accounts, savings accounts, or certificates of deposit. Those are all clothes that you might consider for your saving goals. Investing company statements may list cash or a money market, stocks, bonds, and mutual funds. Those are clothes for investing. Each type of clothes will be covered in depth, but for now, make a list. A template is offered in the review section.

This inventory is the starting point for all you hope to accomplish, so take time to do it. Just as with shopping for clothes, knowing what you have makes your future choices not only easier but also better. You may even be able to complete your outfit with fewer dollars.

REVIEW

1. What is the difference between a STORE and a CLOSET? Give an example of each.

2. What is the maximum dollar amount of insurance coverage per ownership category at a saving store under FDIC and NCUSIF insurance?

3. What is the maximum dollar amount of insurance coverage per customer for lost or missing cash and securities/clothes from a brokerage account/closet? What part of that covers cash?

4. Use this template example to list all the clothes in your existing closets. Each variety of clothes will be covered in depth.

Inventory Of Clothes In My Closets		
Savings Stores	**Clothes in My Closet**	**Value**
ABC Bank	Money Market	$100
	Savings Account	$500
DEF Credit Union	Certificate of Deposit	$1,000
Investing Stores		
UVW Broker-Dealer	Money Market	$5
	Stocks	$6,000
	Bonds	$4,000
	Mutual Funds	$2,000
XYZ Company Retirement	Mutual Funds	$5,000
	TOTAL	**$18,605**

CHAPTER SEVEN:

CLOTHES FOR SAVING

BEFORE YOU SHOP FOR CLOTHES meant for saving, there is a piece of clothing that is not a good fit, and you need to remove it from consideration. A checking account is a type of product that holds money you can access easily via check or debit card. If you earn a wage or salary, your pay is probably deposited directly into a checking account at a bank or credit union. Even if it pays a low rate of interest on your balance, a checking account is **not** a good place for your savings. Why? It is too accessible. Saving requires patience, even though the funds are meant to cover short-term goals. The purpose of a checking account is to pay for everyday transactions. Do not mix funds for saving with funds in your checking account. So then, what kinds of products/clothes are good for saving?

WHAT ARE COMMON WAYS TO SAVE?

First, remember that stores for saving are banks, thrifts, and credit unions. If you need to review their differences, please reread Chapter Five.

What clothes are appropriate for saving? If you have a short-term goal and you want your money to earn interest but do **not** want the risk that you will lose any of the amount that you save (the principal), a *money market account*, a *savings account*, or *certificate of deposit* are all appropriate. (Although money market accounts and savings accounts are commonly called "accounts," for our purposes, they are savings **clothes** offered by savings stores.) A money market account or savings account is also a good place to park your emergency funds, the money set aside for an unexpected need such as the loss of income due to the COVID-19 pandemic.

MONEY MARKET AND SAVINGS ACCOUNTS/CLOTHES

If you choose a money market account, you can expect to easily move money both in and out of the account with few restrictions. Some money market accounts even have check-writing privileges or a debit card, but if you are using this product for saving, you must resist the temptation to use those features until you reach your saving goal. The rate of interest—what the savings store pays you for the use of your money—will change from time to time. The interest will be added to your account balance periodically, usually monthly.

A savings account may pay a higher rate of interest than a money market account, and the rate will change less frequently; however, a savings account typically has more restrictions. The number of times you can take money out of the account each year may be limited, for example, and savings accounts have no checks and no debit card. Again, the interest you earn will be added to the account regularly.

Compare the rates of interest and any restrictions before choosing between a money market and a savings account. If the information is not readily available, ask.

CERTIFICATES OF DEPOSIT

You may also want to consider a certificate of deposit (CD) for saving. A CD is a type of deposit locked in for a specific time, from three months to several years, usually with a fixed rate of interest. The interest you earn on a CD should be higher than either a money market account or a savings account because your money will not be accessible until the date the CD matures. The *maturity* of the CD is set at purchase; therefore, CDs are good places to put funds if the money will be needed on a specific date. For example, imagine that your grandmother gave you $1,000 for your birthday, and you intend to use it for a vacation trip in one year. You want to put the gift in a safe place where you will not be tempted to use it for anything else, so you decide to purchase a $1,000 *face value* CD for one year. The best rate of interest that you find for a one-year CD is 1.50%. At maturity, you will receive $1,015: the principal or face value, $1,000, plus the interest earned, $15. Some CDs pay interest more frequently, so be sure to ask.

Remember, money market accounts, savings accounts, and CDs are clothes issued by savings stores, so they are covered by the insurance of that store—FDIC or NCUSIF. Some savings stores post their CD rates online to attract a wider group of buyers. If you choose to go that route, confirm the insurance coverage, and make sure you understand any fees or restrictions. Also, do not buy a CD at a *premium* (pay a price over its face value), as the premium portion is not covered by insurance.

Even though I do not recommend combining money set aside for saving and money set aside for investing, you may be able to earn a higher rate of interest on a CD purchased through a broker-age account. There are important differences if you do, however.

SHOULD I PURCHASE A CD THROUGH A BROKER-DEALER?

First, broker-dealers do not **issue** CDs; they sell CDs issued by savings stores. Insurance coverage is provided by the CD issuer—the bank or thrift institution. For insurance coverage, it does not matter if you buy the CD directly from the bank or if you buy the CD through a broker-dealer. The ownership rules for insurance coverage still apply.

If you purchase a CD through a broker, the broker may charge you a transaction or other type of fee. Why? Since brokerage firms do not issue CDs but instead sell CDs issued by banks and thrift institutions from all over the U.S., a transaction fee or handling fee is how the broker-dealer covers its costs.

WHAT IF I NEED MY CD MONEY
BEFORE ITS MATURITY?

There is another difference between CDs purchased through a broker-dealer and those purchased directly from a bank, and this comes into play if you need your money prior to the maturity of the CD.

If the CD was purchased through a broker-dealer, the CD will likely be "put out for bid" in the market. The bidding process works kind of like a silent auction. Bidders will offer a specific dollar amount for your CD, and you may receive less than the CD's face value (also called *par value*), your principal purchase amount. You will, however, receive the full amount of interest that you earned up until the date of the sale. Again, the broker-dealer may charge transaction fees or other fees on the sale.

If you purchased your CD directly from a bank, the bank will buy it back at face value, but you may incur an *early withdrawal penalty*, which can be substantial. In either case, you will likely be penalized if you need your money before the maturity of the CD, so try to match the maturity with the point in time you need the money.

If you are somewhat unsure of the date you will need the money, you might consider a CD *ladder*. Just as a ladder has several rungs, a CD ladder has several maturities. You might put part of the money meant for your wedding, whose date is set a year from now, in a CD that matures in one year, part in a CD that matures in six months, part in a CD that matures in two months, and the rest in a money market account. As wedding expenses arise—the bridal gown, venue, flowers, cake, etc.—the money is safe, is earning interest, and will be available when you need it.

It is important to fully understand savings clothes and their associated costs, fees, or penalties. If the information is not readily available, ask. Then, take advantage of correct ownership titling to safeguard your money and assure full insurance coverage. If you have a very large amount of money for short-term goals, over the limit of insurance coverage, it is a good idea to spread your funds among multiple banks, credit unions, or thrift institutions. Doing this will make sure you have full insurance coverage in the event of an insolvency of one of them. You want your clothes to be safe.

REVIEW

1. Which piece of clothing is not good for saving? Why?

2. What pieces of clothing/products are good for saving?

3. What are the differences between money market and savings accounts?

4. Which savings product has a fixed maturity so is less flexible?

5. What is a CD ladder?

6. What are the differences between buying a CD directly from a bank or thrift institution and buying a CD through a broker?

CHAPTER EIGHT:

CLOTHES FOR INVESTING

BECAUSE INVESTING IS FOR LONG-TERM goals, different clothes are appropriate. That said, a money market account may be part of a brokerage account because it is used as a temporary parking place when you deposit money to make a purchase or between sales and subsequent purchases. Money earned on your investments (interest and dividend payments) will also be placed in the money market account. Funds flow freely in and out as needed, and interest is typically earned on any balance.

(Note: A money market account is NOT the same as a *money market mutual fund*. A money market mutual fund requires a purchase/sale of a specific dollar amount or number of shares;

usually one dollar equals one share. A money market mutual fund manager invests in liquid, short-term fixed income instruments, cash, and cash equivalents. Although rare, the dollar price per share of a money market mutual fund could drop below $1.)

For a **basic** investment outfit, the types of clothes from which to choose include stocks and bonds, or mutual funds and *exchange-traded funds* (ETFs) which are composed of stocks and bonds. Stocks and bonds have very different characteristics, and most outfits will include both. In the investing world, stocks, bonds, and cash are the three main asset classes. Asset classes are groups of securities with similar characteristics which cause them to behave similarly in the markets. What are the main differences between stocks and bonds?

STOCKS/EQUITIES

Common stock is what people usually think of when they think of investing, and it is the kind of stock that is appropriate for a basic investment outfit. As part of your outfit, stocks are the tops—sweaters, blouses, T-shirts, etc. Stock represents ownership of, or *equity* in, a company, and the amount of your ownership is reflected by the number of shares. When you own a share of IBM stock, you are a part-owner of IBM. Owners or shareholders **may** get payments from the profits of the company. Those payments are called *stock dividends*. If a company comes on bad times, it may cut its stock dividend or do away with it entirely. Lots more about stock later.

Stock is purchased and sold on a *stock exchange*, so instructions, or *orders*, must be placed with a broker-dealer who is a member of the exchange. The exchange sets the trading hours.

The New York Stock Exchange, for example, is open weekdays from 9:30 a.m. to 4:00 p.m. EST. The best way for beginners to own stock is through a stock mutual fund or exchange-traded fund (ETF). Why? Because mutual funds and ETFs typically hold many, many different stocks. That way, your future does not ride on just one or two or three companies. The added diversity of owning many companies and types of companies reduces risk.

BONDS/FIXED INCOME

Bonds represent the debt of a company, an IOU, or a loan. For your investment outfit, bonds are the bottoms—pants, capris, skirts, etc. When you own a bond, you are a lender to that company. Let's say that Intel wants to build a new factory in the U.S. They could go to their bank or another financial partner to borrow the money. Instead of borrowing funds through those methods, a company might choose to go directly to the general public and ask you, and many others, to lend them the money to build the plant. They do that by issuing bonds. Why would you want to lend Intel, or another company, money? Because during the time Intel has the use of your money, you will be paid interest. Plus, at a designated time in the future, Intel will return all the money borrowed from you—the principal. Bonds are sometimes called *fixed income* because the amount of interest you earn is typically a fixed rate or percentage, for example, Intel 2.875% maturing 05/11/2024. This bond pays owners 2.875% annually on the face value of their investment and will return the entire face value on May 11, 2024. Although bonds are issued with an annual rate of interest, interest payments are usually split so bondholders receive half semi-annually.

If Intel has difficult financial times, *bondholders* will be paid before *stockholders*. Bonds are debt, a liability of the company, and debts get paid before any funds are distributed to stockholders, the owners.

Some bonds are traded on an exchange, but most are traded "over-the-counter." *Over-the-counter markets* are those in which trades take place directly between two parties without the use of a central exchange. Because of the way they trade and for added diversity, the best way for beginning investors to buy bonds is via a bond mutual fund or ETF. Then you will be part-owner of many different bonds, and once again, diversity lowers risk.

CONCENTRATION

When you made a list of what you already have in your closets, was there a lot of one stock? That is easy to do if you like a company and purchased its stock in several different closets or if you work for a company that offers a discount on purchases of its own stock. However, having too much of one stock can work against you, and that is called *concentration risk*. A rule of thumb says that you should hold no more than 5% of any one stock—Amazon, for example—in your **combined** investment closets.

If you find that you own too much of one stock, is it possible for you to reduce the amount over time without taking large capital gains? Capital gains are the difference between the purchase cost and the sale proceeds. If your stock has been held for a long time, it has likely appreciated in value and, if held in a *taxable account* (a closet in which any income from the clothes held in the closet is subject to tax), you will pay capital gains tax on the net gains—the profit from the sale. Long-term capital gains are taxed at a lower rate than the tax rate for personal income. To qualify for the long-term capital gains tax rate, the stock, bond, or other investment must be held for **over** a year. Taxes are important because they reduce your return, so always check the purchase *trade date*, the beginning of the holding period, before you sell to try to get past the one-year mark.

Capital gains tax will not be assessed on a sale if the stock or other investment is held in an IRA, 401(k), or *other tax-advantaged account* (closet in which tax payment on income is postponed until funds are removed from the closet). Those closets have special tax rules to encourage saving for the long term. The most common taxable and tax-advantaged accounts/closets are listed in Part Four.

If you choose not to reduce your concentrated holding and understand the risk to your portfolio, be sure to not only monitor the company but also its industry or *sector*. Disney is part of the entertainment industry and communication services sector, so news that affects those broad categories may affect Disney as well, and economic news may affect all: the industry, the sector, and the company. If you are employed by or deeply attached to a company, ask someone who is not emotionally attached to monitor the stock. For example, if Aunt Jane gave you Disney stock because both of you **love** Disney, Aunt Jane is not the best person to help you review your portfolio that is mainly Disney stock. Both you and Aunt Jane are emotionally attached to that security.

The stock portion of a portfolio can also be concentrated if the stocks, although not individually concentrated, are concentrated in one industry or sector. If you own a technology mutual fund plus Microsoft, Sony, and Apple stock, your portfolio may be concentrated. Your return will then rise and fall with the technology industry. An example of the downside of industry concentration happened in the late 1990s when the number of internet company startups exploded, and investment in their stocks soared. As internet stock valuations reached unreasonable levels—some companies did not generate revenue, some made no profit, and some did not even have a product—the so-called dot-com bubble burst.

Concentration risk pertains to **stock** in a portfolio. This rule does not apply to money market accounts, CDs, and savings accounts used for short-term saving. It can apply to mutual funds and exchange-traded funds, however. To assess the concentration risk of mutual funds or exchange-traded funds, compare the top holdings. Yahoo Finance, under the Holdings tab, lists not only the top ten holdings but also the sector weights of a mutual fund or ETF. Similar information may be found on websites of brokerage firms or the fund or ETF itself. If you are willing to pay a membership fee, Morningstar has a mutual fund instant X-ray tool for a more comprehensive analysis of combined fund characteristics.

The types of clothes that are appropriate for a basic investment outfit are stocks and bonds combined with money markets and cash. However, it is difficult for a beginning investor to buy enough of each to spread out the risk. A way to combine stocks and bonds to create the most diverse wardrobe with the least amount of money is to use mutual funds or exchange-traded funds, and a wise shopper will focus on those choices.

REVIEW

1. What are the three main asset classes?

2. What is stock? What is someone who owns stock called? If a payment is made to an owner, what is that called?

3. What is a bond? How are bond owners paid?

4. How are stocks and bonds alike? How are they different?

5. What is concentration risk? Why is it important?

SAMPLE CONCENTRATION ANALYSIS

Use the statements you gathered for your existing closets. From those statements, create a list of stocks, **only stocks**, along with the current market value for each stock. The stock holdings should be clearly labeled and easy to identify.

Next, if a stock appears in more than one closet, as Apple and Amazon do in the following example, combine the value of each stock from all closets. Compare the combined value to the total value of your entire investment portfolio, in this case $460,000. In the example, not all portfolio assets are stock. The bulk of the portfolio is invested in mutual funds and ETFs.

STOCK CONCENTRATION EVALUATOR		
	Market Value $	Sector
Connie's Individual Account		
Apple	$5,000	Technology
Amazon	$4,000	Consumer Cyclical
Facebook	$3,000	Communication Services
Connie's IRA Account		
Apple	$8,000	Technology
Starbucks	$7,000	Consumer Cyclical
Connie's Employee Stock Account		
Amazon	$10,000	Consumer Cyclical
David's 401(k)		
Intel	$8,000	Technology
Market Value of Other Assets	$415,000	
Total Value of All Assets	$460,000	

The market value of the two holdings of Apple is $13,000. The combined value of the two holdings of Amazon is $14,000. Apple is 2.8% and Amazon is 3% of the total value of the entire portfolio. No stock has a current market value of 5% (or more) of the combined household portfolio. If, however, any of Connie's mutual funds or ETFs also hold the stocks listed, she may already have a concentration.

Imagine that it is a year from now, and the total portfolio is now worth $480,000. Connie purchased more Amazon stock in her employee stock account/closet, and Amazon also appreciated in value. Now Amazon's total value in the household portfolio is $26,000, and that is 5.4% of the portfolio. Connie should either cut back future purchases of Amazon stock in her employee stock account/closet or sell some Amazon stock in her *individual account*/closet. Before she does the latter, she will determine the potential capital gain, so she does not have a tax surprise.

If Connie owns a technology mutual fund with a value of $10,000, there is a different kind of concentration. What is it?

CHAPTER NINE:

CLOTHES FOR A BASIC OUTFIT

ARE YOU A BUSY PROFESSIONAL, a stay-at-home mom, or someone who's just started shopping for a financial wardrobe? If so, then an option to create an outfit that takes as little of your time as possible will fit you to a T. Mutual funds and exchange-traded funds (ETFs) match that criterion. Why? Because your investment dollars purchase many more securities (stocks, bonds, or both combined). What is the advantage of that? If you focus your investment in the stock of one company, your portfolio will go up and down with that company's stock. That movement is normal and expected. However, owning one stock or only a few increases the possibility that you may need to sell all or part at a loss when the stock is down. If, on the other hand, you own pieces of hundreds of companies in diverse sectors and industries, or you own the debt of many companies through a mutual fund or ETF, that risk is spread out. That is called *diversification*.

Mutual funds and exchange-traded funds may perform better, or worse, than the stock of a single company or the bond of one issuer, but the risk of loss from an unexpected sale is less. Plus, picking a single stock winner is very difficult to do consistently over time. Diversification reduces risk. **Mutual funds and ETFs have lots of advantages for a beginning investor.**

MUTUAL FUNDS

What are mutual funds? Simplistically, hundreds of people pool their money and find an investment company with a professional manager who selects the securities to be included in the fund. Let's say you want to buy a mutual fund invested in large U.S. company stocks. You look for an investment company with a good professional manager, and you invest $1,000. Your ownership is represented in shares of the mutual fund; however, you do not have a say in what the manager of the fund buys. You know she will buy large companies that are domiciled in the U.S. because she is required to follow the mandate or purpose of the fund stated in its *prospectus*, the document filed with the *Securities and Exchange Commission* (SEC) when the fund was created.

PROCESS OF MUTUAL FUND INVESTMENT

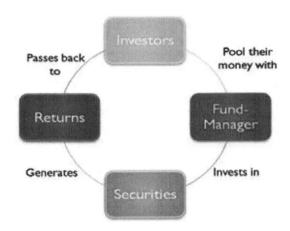

Source: Surbhi, S. (2018, December 13) Process of Mutual Fund Investment. Retrieved from https://keydifferences. com/difference-between-mutual-fund-and-etf.html

How can you get information about mutual funds and tell if the manager is doing a good job? Independent companies track mutual fund performance along with other important information about a fund: its purpose, its holdings, how long it has been in existence, biographies of the managers, etc. The best-known company that tracks mutual fund performance is Morningstar. You can compare information about mutual funds on Morningstar's website, **morningstar.com**, with a subscription, but you can also find mutual fund information on other websites. BigCharts/ MarketWatch and Yahoo Finance are two that are well known. You could also search one of the major broker-dealer websites and select the research function.

Just remember to compare apples to apples. For example, compare a mutual fund that invests in U.S. large company stock to another that also invests in U.S. large company stock, not to one that invests in *international stocks* or even U.S. small company stocks. That is like comparing the price of a warm sweater to the price of a tank top and choosing one just because it costs less. The sweater is more appropriate in the winter and the tank top in the summer. They serve different purposes.

You can also track the daily performance of a mutual fund online by checking the market value per share of the mutual fund. Both Yahoo Finance and BigCharts/MarketWatch allow you to set up a free account and enter your personal holdings. Then you can see if the price is up or down from where you purchased your shares. Many cell phones also have a stock app that includes mutual funds and ETFs.

MUTUAL FUNDS WITH ACTIVE MANAGEMENT

The mutual fund described earlier uses *active management*. The selection of securities to go into the mutual fund is made deliberately. Staff members review companies being considered for investment—in the prior case, all U.S. companies designated as large. Then the managers decide which companies they think will do the best, and they buy the stock of those companies. If, in the constant monitoring of those companies and other potential candidates, they decide that changes are necessary, the mutual fund managers will make those changes without checking with shareholders, the investors/owners.

MUTUAL FUNDS WITH PASSIVE MANAGEMENT

Another type of mutual fund uses a different management approach. It is called *passive management* because the managers do not choose which securities to include. They typically copy, or mirror, an *index* and include all or most of the companies in that index. Using our previous example, instead of reviewing and selecting certain U.S. large companies based on their expected performance, the manager of an S&P 500 Index Fund will select **all** the companies in the *S&P 500 Index*, which includes 500 large U.S. publicly traded companies. There is no active decision by fund managers of the stocks or bonds to be included; the managers copy the index.

People are often confused when they buy an index mutual fund. They are not actually buying the index. They are buying a mutual fund that replicates, or copies, the index. That is important because the return of the mutual fund will typically be slightly lower than the stated return of the index. Why? Because the operating costs of the mutual fund must be subtracted before its return is computed.

WHICH IS BETTER, ACTIVE OR PASSIVE?

Which type of mutual fund is better: active or passive? Do you prefer the guarantee of average market performance or the chance of outperformance? Although an active manager is trying to outperform the market and may do so for a few years, in general, it is difficult for her to outperform over long periods of time. "Over the past 10 years, fewer than one in 10 actively managed *blue-chip stock* funds have outperformed comparable index funds and only about 20% [of] small-company stock funds have done so."[10] Index funds have an operating cost advantage because it is not necessary to hire a large staff to select appropriate securities. You may decide you like one or the other or perhaps a combination of both active and passive management. There is no right or wrong answer.

COMMON FEATURES

Purchases and sales of mutual funds we previously discussed, both actively and passively managed, are placed directly with the mutual fund company, not through an exchange. Mutual funds are priced once a day after market close. The closing market price of each stock or bond in the fund is added together, the liabilities of the mutual fund (its expenses and operating costs) are deducted, that amount is divided by the number of shares outstanding, and the result is the *net asset value or* NAV. When you place an order to buy or sell a mutual fund, you will not know the exact price because trade orders must be placed **before** market close, and the pricing of mutual funds takes place **after** market close. The money to pay for the mutual fund will be taken out of (or if it's a sale, be put into) your account/closet the next business day, in most cases. Mutual funds vary in the minimum amount you need to invest. An initial investment is usually $2,500 to $3,000 but can be as low as $500. Subsequent investments are much less, $50 or $100, for example. You can also set up for dollar cost averaging, automatic investments at regular intervals, with most mutual funds.

EXCHANGE-TRADED FUNDS

Since the 1990s, another mutual-fund-like investment product has become popular, exchange-traded funds or ETFs. ETFs contain many different securities, like mutual funds, but they are not sold directly by mutual fund companies. Instead, ETFs are purchased and sold via a stock exchange, and you must place trades to buy or sell through a brokerage account/closet like you do stock. Although that typically means you would pay a *sales charge or commission* to a broker, many firms now offer free trades for some ETFs (and stocks, too). ETFs started as a way to buy and sell index mutual funds during a trading day instead of waiting until market close. There are now hundreds of ETFs through which you can buy all types of securities, including stocks and bonds, and some ETFs even use active management. More and more actively managed ETFs enter the market each year.

In addition to the way they trade, ETFs and mutual funds also differ in how their price is set. ETFs trade all day long, so the market value of the ETF is adjusting on an ongoing basis to the changes in the market price of the underlying stocks and bonds. Although it adjusts quickly, the price of an ETF may occasionally be more or less than its NAV. Another difference is in the amount of money required for an investment. Where mutual funds set a minimum purchase and reinvestment amount, you can buy as little as one share of an ETF. Also, ETFs usually have lower, sometimes much lower, operating expenses than a comparable mutual fund. And due to the structure of an ETF, it is more tax-efficient than a mutual fund.

Mutual funds and exchange-traded funds are the best choices for a basic investment outfit. Both provide a wide selection of styles, are professionally managed, and offer diversity among many stocks and bonds with one investment. Not only do mutual funds and ETFs provide diversification, which reduces risk (as long as concentration is monitored regularly), but they also give you a choice of active and passive management.

REVIEW

1. What is a mutual fund?

2. How are active and passive management different?

3. What is an exchange-traded fund? How is it different from a mutual fund? How is it the same?

4. Why are mutual funds and ETFs the best choice for a basic investment outfit?

CHAPTER TEN:

ARE THERE OTHER EXPENSES?

IN ADDITION TO THE COST OF THE INVESTMENT (stock, bond, mutual fund), there may be fees associated with a purchase or sale. When you shop for clothes, you may pay sales tax and, if you purchase online, you may pay shipping fees. Fees are an essential consideration. The more you pay in fees and other charges, the less you have available to invest, and that affects how quickly you reach your goals.

Although it may be relatively easy to determine the costs associated with saving (short term), investing (long term) may be a bit more difficult because of the varied options. The costs to invest, as in shopping for a wardrobe, will be affected by both your goals (how much you have available to invest), where you go to make your purchases (which store you choose), and your choice of investments (the clothes you select).

MUTUAL FUND EXPENSES

All mutual funds incur expenses. The fund must pay the professional investment managers along with bookkeepers, marketing and sales professionals, and human resource personnel. The fund must also cover the cost of supplies, offices, and utilities, for example. There is a way to measure the expenses of a mutual fund in relationship to its assets—the market value of the securities in the fund. The relationship is expressed as a ratio: the total annual cost or expense as a percentage of total assets. This is called the *Operating Expense Ratio* (OER), and it is readily available. It is published. The lower the OER compared to similar options, the better. According to Morningstar, asset-weighted fund fees have dropped substantially, from an average of 0.87% to 0.45% over the past twenty years. That is a good thing for investors.

From our previous discussion, you will remember that index mutual funds and ETFs will typically have lower operating expenses. Fee wars have pushed expenses lower, and some index funds have as low as 0.03% OER. Fidelity ZERO mutual funds charge no operating expenses. That makes it even more important to compare. Lower operating expenses mean more of your money goes to work for you.

Mutual funds may put additional restrictions on certain funds or charge a fee in some cases. Common ones are:

- *redemption fees or short-term trading fees*: fees meant to discourage selling too quickly

- *minimum hold time*: a length of time a mutual fund may require you to hold the fund before you can sell

- *front-end or back-end loads*: a commission or sales charge assessed at initial purchase (front-end) or sale (back-end)

The *Financial Industry Regulatory Authority* (FINRA) Fund Analyzer at **finra.org** is a free tool to help investors sort and compare mutual funds and ETFs and understand the impact of fees and potential discounts. It also does the math to show how fees and expenses impact the value of an investment over time. (Select "For Investors" and then "Tools and Calculators.")

BROKERAGE ACCOUNT FEES

Check to see what charges or fees are involved before you invest with a brokerage firm. Are those costs assessed annually, quarterly, or with each transaction? Here are common ones:

- *administrative or custodial fees*: fees to cover the cost of record keeping, reporting, and safekeeping

- sales charges/loads or commissions: charges assessed with the purchase or sale of certain products/clothes

- advisory fees: cost of professional advice or ongoing management

Some of these expenses are reported separately and are readily available, and some take a little more work to find. Some are charges associated with a particular piece of clothing, and some are associated with the broker or broker-dealer firm—the store. **Ask how you will be charged and what fees and expenses to expect. This is important!** To maximize your success, you want as much of your investable dollars to be used to purchase investments/clothes and not to pay fees and cover expenses.

REVIEW

1. Describe typical mutual fund expenses.

2. Describe typical brokerage account fees.

3. Why is it important to minimize fees and expenses?

PART
THREE

At this point, you should be familiar with the stores, closets, and clothes for both saving and investing. If you need to review, Chapter Five covers stores, Chapter Six covers closets, and saving and investing clothes are described in Chapters Seven, Eight, and Nine.

Now it is time to focus on how to put saving and investing clothes together to complete a basic investment outfit. The type of clothes that are best for a basic investment outfit are mutual funds or ETFs. Why? Because you will own many, many different stocks and/or bonds with each mutual fund or ETF purchase, and that reduces risk. Are you ready?

CHAPTER ELEVEN:
THE FOUNDATION

A FOUNDATION IS A STARTING POINT. It is the underlying base or ground upon which something is built. What is the foundation for your investment outfit? It is your underwear.

Some of you choose to wear a sexy bra and panties and some are more comfortable with full coverage. You know what is right for you. But what happens if you choose not to wear any underwear? Well, there is the possibility that, at some point, you could be exposed and maybe embarrass yourself. It is a risk.

Your investment outfit, your portfolio, runs the same risk. The foundation of your portfolio is your emergency fund. What is an emergency fund? It is money set aside for the unknown surprise. According to a 2018 study by the Federal Reserve, 40% of U.S. households would struggle to pay for a $400 unexpected expense.[11] The amount you choose to set aside for emergencies depends on what other resources you have and how quickly you could sell them to create cash. An emergency fund, like underwear, keeps you from being exposed at the worst possible time. It can give you a sense of security and comfort. It is the starting point for the rest of your outfit.

HOW MUCH SHOULD BE IN MY EMERGENCY FUND?

How do you know how much to set aside for emergencies? The rule of thumb is three to six months of living expenses: costs that must be met each month to have a place to live, food to eat, and a way to get to work. In the Chapter Two review, you computed a value for your emergency fund. (See Chapter Two, Question #1.)

Here is an example of an emergency fund calculation using the budget of a family of four with an income of $40,000 and monthly expenses of $2,200.[12]

Mortgage/Rent	$850
Electric/Gas/Water/Sewer	$115
TV/Phone/Internet	$100

This family has no car payment or credit card balance. They add their average monthly expenses for groceries, transportation, and insurance.

Groceries/Personal/Household	$550
Transportation	$120
Insurance and Healthcare	$80

The emergency fund does not include money for eating out or clothing or entertainment, which are extra or discretionary expenses. For the household just described the monthly total for necessary expenses to be covered by an emergency fund is $1,815. If they decide to save enough to cover necessary expenses for three to six months, an emergency fund somewhere between $5,445 and $10,890 is appropriate.

How does that compare with other households? A recent article in *The New York Times Magazine* profiled expenditures of six families from across the country during the COVID-19 pandemic.[13] The households varied from two people to eight people, and total **monthly** expenses ranged from $4,815 to $11,269. The highest expenses were for a couple living in California with a new baby, a large payment for education loans, sizable donations, and a contribution to a 401(k). The next highest was the family of eight with $9,765 in monthly expenses. Their expenses also included donations, gifts, and a large contribution to savings. My quick calculation of emergency fund expenses for the eight families ranged from $3,300 to $6,025 **per month**. That is substantially higher than the expenses of the family of four previously mentioned. Therefore, each of these families would need a much larger emergency fund—a minimum of $9,900 to $18,075.

In one study, economists Emily Gallagher and Jorge Sabat took an in-depth look and found a realistic emergency fund for **low-income** households was about $2,500.[14] Their data did not look at middle- or high-income households, however. If yours is a middle-income household, as the example of the family of four with a household income of $40,000, you would expect to at least double the $2,500 to $5,000, and that approaches the minimum amount indicated by the rule of thumb, $5,445. But if your monthly expenses are closer to one of the families profiled in the *Times* article, your emergency fund should be substantially larger.

What is realistic for you and your household? Only you will know what adjustments must be made. You may be single, married but have no children, or have many children. If your children are young, groceries may not be as big a part of your monthly expenses as when they are teenagers. You may live in an area where the cost of living is very high. Does someone in your household have critical medical needs that must be met? Are there others outside of your immediate household that depend on you for financial support? All these factors will affect the size of your emergency fund.

Now, you may be the kind of person who chooses to go without an emergency fund. You will not be carted away. However, it is a risk, and it should be a conscious decision. Emergency funds should be put into a SAVING type of closet, **not invested in the stock or bond markets**. You do not know when an emergency may arise, and you want to be able to get to that money quickly and easily without the possibility of loss. During the COVID-19 pandemic, an emergency fund would have kept many people from worry and stress, or at least eased their anxiety.

REVIEW

1. What is an emergency fund?

2. What should an emergency fund cover?

3. What other factors affect the amount of an emergency fund?

4. What is a safe place for your emergency fund?

5. Review the emergency fund computation you did in Chapter Two. Using a target of three months of living expenses, do you need to make any adjustments to the dollar amount of your emergency fund?

CHAPTER TWELVE:

SHOES

EVEN FOR THOSE WHO LOVE TO GO BAREFOOT, shoes are an essential part of an outfit. From flip-flops to classic pumps to running shoes to spike heels, they have a purpose. Shoes complete your look, but more importantly, they serve a function, such as the support needed for running. If I saw nothing but your shoes, I would likely get a sense of the look of the rest of your outfit. Shoes are also important for your general well-being. Ill-fitting shoes may make you miserable, while you may even forget you have on comfortable shoes. In any case, they bring your outfit together.

What is comparable to shoes for an investment portfolio? It is the **asset allocation**–the target percentage of stocks and bonds, which we discussed in Chapter Four. In the case of a portfolio, as with shoes, the allocation supports the purpose of the portfolio. If it is the right fit, you will forget about it. However, if it's ill-fitting, it will cause you misery and many sleepless nights.

Review the results of the portfolio allocation exercise you completed as part of the Chapter Four review questions. You selected a particular mix of stocks and bonds: 70% stock and 30% bonds, for example. Use that as your target asset allocation for your investment outfit.

WHEN SHOULD I CHANGE MY SHOE STYLE?

If your parents start investing for you when you are a small child, they are likely to be very aggressive, maybe even allocate 100% to stock. They let you go barefoot. The risk is that you stub your toe or step on a rock, but as parents know, children are typically fast to recover. With a child's portfolio, if the stock market goes down, there is typically time to recover before the money is needed. If that portfolio is meant to pay for the cost of education, then the shoes typically become more conventional and functional the closer you get to college or tech school. The allocation of stock in a portfolio lessens, and bonds and cash become greater.

A similar situation occurs when you get close to retirement–you want less volatility, which means a more conservative shoe style. But, at the same time, you need to cover an ever-growing cost of living that includes medical expenses. You also want to be able to do all the things you planned for retirement: travel, play golf, take up a new hobby, or spend time with the grandkids. However, unlike education, retirement may last ten, twenty, or more years. If you want to not only keep up with inflation but also continue to grow your nest egg, it is imperative that you keep part of your portfolio invested in stock. Depending on your life expectancy, health, and other income sources, a delay to any asset allocation change may be appropriate until later in retirement–keep the shoes you currently use for a while.

In between childhood and retirement, however, shoes run the gamut. Many women in midlife, the earning years, want shoes that are both functional and fashionable, but not too extreme–maybe pumps or wedges or even boots. This is like an allocation of stock to bonds in the middle ranges from 60/40 to 50/50 to 40/60. However, let's say you like the idea of spike heels, so you invest in lots of stock and little in bonds. You could wear your heels with a T-shirt and jeans, or you could wear them with a fancy dress to a dance. In any case, it isn't likely that you will wear those heels all the time. You would not wear them for running, for example. Their use is limited.

Over your lifetime, you will find the same with your portfolio. An aggressive stance in a portfolio, a high percentage of stock, will result in more volatility. At times, that allocation isn't what you want or isn't appropriate. Maybe you become a widow or go through a divorce. At those times, you may desire more stability and, therefore, a more conservative allocation to your portfolio–more bonds. You choose different shoes. Reassess your risk tolerance at those times. Even when life is going smoothly, it's a good idea to reassess your allocation no less than every five years. However, changes to a target allocation typically occur only a handful of times in your investing lifetime.

Especially when it comes to your asset allocation, resist the temptation to do what your sister or best friend is doing. After all, do you always buy the same style of shoes as them? You are unique, and you have different life circumstances than anyone else. You may be single or married, have children, have a career outside the home, and earn more or less than others, but if you are reading this book, you are likely just starting to invest. The reasons that you are investing and the time until you need the money affect the amount of risk for your portfolio.

WHAT DOES IT MEAN TO REBALANCE?

In addition to a conscious change in allocation for life changes, your allocation will also adjust with market movement. Because the price of clothes in both the stock and bond markets is constantly moving up and down, some pieces of your outfit will rise in value, and some will decrease. Over time, that rise and fall can affect your asset allocation. For example, let's say your target allocation is 60% stock and 40% bonds. If you find that the stock portion of your outfit has grown to 68% while the bond portion decreased to 32%, it is time to *rebalance* your outfit. That is different from changing your target allocation. **A rebalance is the process of bringing your outfit back to its target.** In the example, the target has not changed; it is still 60% stock and 40% bonds. Think of rebalancing as washing or polishing or putting new heels on your shoes. Your goal is to bring your shoes back to their original luster. Plan to rebalance annually and when there are major market moves.

How do you make your shoes shine again? You could sell the overweight piece and buy the underweight piece. That may not be wise, however, especially if your clothes are in a taxable account. Sales in a taxable closet could trigger capital gains, which are subject to tax (see Chapter Eight). Another alternative, using the earlier example, would be to stop buying tops (stock) and only add to bottoms (bonds). Or you could buy both but overweight the bond piece instead of the stock piece. These alternatives might take more time to get to your target allocation, but they could also keep you from unintended tax consequences. By the way, the same methods you use to rebalance can also be used when you change your target allocation.

WHY ARE SHOES IMPORTANT?

Shoes are the most important choice that you will make in dressing your naked portfolio! Studies have shown that asset allocation has more to do with successfully meeting your goals than any other decision. The proper allocation keeps you invested in both good and bad market conditions. Your shoes are important, and as you are undoubtedly aware, they can cause you a great deal of pain, or they can make life easier. The wrong allocation may keep you awake at night, but you won't even feel your shoes when the allocation is right.

REVIEW

1. Review your risk tolerance assessment from Chapter Four. What asset allocation did it recommend for you?

2. Why are shoes (asset allocation) important?

3. When should you change your shoe style?

4. What tool will help you decide what your new shoe style should be?

5. What is the difference between changing your shoe style (your target asset allocation) and shining your shoes (rebalancing)?

6. What methods can you use to both rebalance and change your asset allocation?

CHAPTER THIRTEEN:

TOPS

WHAT ARE YOU WEARING TODAY? Are you comfortable? Do you like to dress up or dress down? Are you conservative with your clothes, or do you wear the latest fashion and look forward to the chance to try something new? Do you like to mix it up and create new combinations for variety? Have you worn the same hairstyle for years, or do you change it every few months?

You can choose from hundreds of mutual fund and ETF options, just as you can choose from hundreds of articles of clothing to buy a new outfit. You might prefer a dress, a skirt and top, or jeans and a T-shirt. To help you pick the investment outfit that fits your style, let's look at your fashion options. Stocks and bonds, introduced in Chapter Eight, have different characteristics. Like a blouse and pants, they react differently in their markets. Each brings unique qualities—diversification—to your investment outfit, and together they give insight into your personality.

TOPS: SHIRTS AND BLOUSES

The basic investment outfit equivalent of a top is a domestic (U.S.) stock mutual fund or ETF. What does stock do for your investment outfit? If you wear a new outfit, chances are that your friends will notice your top first and talk about it. They might call it avant-garde, classy, or Western, for example. What color(s) do you choose: bright red, forest green, or yellow? Or do you tend to stick with black and white or pale colors? You might say that this fashion choice can make or break your outfit. It has great potential to make a positive impression, but pick the wrong color or style, and it can also have a downside.

The upside to stock investments can be almost limitless, but there can also be dramatic downturns, as witnessed in 1987, 2000–2001, and 2007–2008. Stocks are typically more volatile than bonds. Because there is more risk, there is also greater potential for return. The more volatility you can weather **and stay invested** in the stock market, the greater the percentage of stock you should own. The goal is to stay covered, not to panic and rip off your top. Review your risk profile from Chapter Four and the discussion in Chapter Twelve. What percentage of stock did it suggest for your investment outfit?

There is almost always a link between risk and return.

What makes the price of a particular stock go up or down? The price of a company's stock is affected by the economy in general (this is called *market or systemic risk*), the company's product or service (are sales good or bad), the outlook for its industry or sector (are people going to the movie theater or choosing other forms of entertainment, for example), and the expected company earnings (future sales), among other factors. Imagine that someone who follows technology stocks just issued a report that suggests Apple's earnings will increase more than previously expected. Investors may rush to buy Apple stock, and that could cause the price to increase. A stock's price may also be affected by supply and demand in the market. When a stock is added to an index, for example, any mutual fund or ETF that tracks that index must add that stock to its portfolio. That could cause the stock's price to increase. It is the opposite when a stock is dropped from an index.

So, what kind of return can you expect from the U.S. stock market? Let's use the S&P 500 Index, which tracks 500 large U.S. companies, as an indication. Remember that you can't invest in an index directly, but you can invest in a mutual fund or ETF that mirrors, or copies, the index.

WHAT KIND OF RETURN CAN I EXPECT FROM STOCK?

Over short time periods, the S&P 500 Index has delivered both very high returns and very low returns. The chart that follows looks at the one, three, five, ten, fifteen, and twenty-year rolling returns of the S&P 500 Index over the forty-year period of January 1979 through December 2019, as an example.

Rolling returns do not go by the calendar year; instead, they look at every one-year, three-year, five-year, etc., time period beginning anew **each month** over the historical time frame selected. Rolling returns give you a picture of how the stock market performs over both good and bad times. You don't get the complete picture when you only look at average returns because the average smooths out the ups and downs.

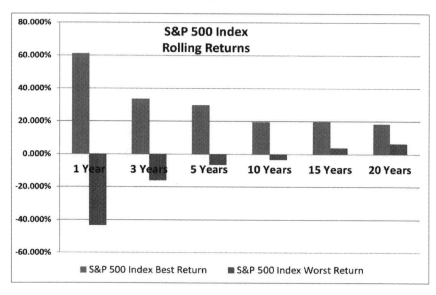

Source: Anspach, Dana, *Control Your Retirement Destiny: Achieving Financial Security Before The Big Transition.* Fort Collins, CO, A Book's Mind, 2016. Chart updated by, and used with permission of, author. Past performance is no guarantee of future results.

ONE-YEAR RETURNS WERE VOLATILE

During the period of January 1979 through December 2019 in the graph, the **worst one-year** rolling time frame delivered a return of -43%. That occurred over the twelve months ending in February 2009.

The **best one-year** index return delivered a positive 61% return, which occurred over the twelve months ending in June 1983. Huge swings can occur over relatively short time frames.

WORST TWENTY-YEAR RETURNS WERE POSITIVE

Using the same historical time frame, if you were a long-term investor, the **worst twenty years** delivered a return of **positive** 5.6% a year. That occurred over the twenty years ending in December 2019. The **best twenty years** delivered a return of positive 18% a year, which occurred over the twenty years ending in March 2000. Both the best and worst twenty-year rolling returns were positive. What does that indicate? **The longer you can stay invested, the greater the possibility of a positive return.**

Always remember that it is **time in the stock market** that will serve you as an investor. **The more time you can stay invested, even over years when the stock market is down, the better your chance of a long-term positive return.** Timing the market, on the other hand (trying to pick the lowest point to buy or the highest point to sell), is extremely difficult. Despite ads that suggest that possibility, even the pros rarely correctly predict the highest or lowest points.

REVIEW

1. What is diversification, and what does it do for an investment portfolio?

2. Why is systemic risk not diversifiable?

3. What do shirts and blouses represent in an investment portfolio, and why?

4. What kind of return can you expect from large-cap U.S. stock?

5. What factors affect the return of stocks?

CHAPTER FOURTEEN:

BOTTOMS

ALTHOUGH AN ESSENTIAL PART of any two-piece outfit, pants or a skirt are less likely to be the focal point. You may like bright floral pants or leggings, which attract attention and can be beautiful. For a basic investment outfit, however, a more conservative choice is best—perhaps a pair of embroidered jeans or a flared skirt. In any case, your pants or skirt combine with a gorgeous top to tell the world who you are. As you continue to select clothes for your investment outfit, domestic (U.S.) bond mutual funds and ETFs will be the equivalent of the pants or skirt.

BOTTOMS: SKIRTS AND PANTS

Bonds trade in higher dollar increments ($1,000, $5,000, $100,000) than stock, so it takes more money to buy enough bonds to get proper diversification. Therefore, bond mutual funds or ETFs, where you are part-owner of hundreds of bond issues, make especially good sense.

What do bond mutual funds do for your investment outfit? Although the price of bonds fluctuates, the degree of fluctuation, or volatility, is usually less than stock, and therefore bonds are considered a more conservative part of your investment outfit. There is more certainty with bonds than with stocks. Except for *junk bonds* (which are low *credit quality*, like short shorts, and not appropriate for a basic investment outfit), you can expect to receive regular interest payments and the return of your principal at maturity. If the issuing company has financial problems, bondholders receive payment before stockholders. Does that sound like less risk than stock? You bet. **When you combine bond mutual funds with stock mutual funds, you make the overall portfolio less volatile.**

WHAT AFFECTS THE PRICE OF BONDS?

Prices of bonds, just like stock, fluctuate with the general condition of the economy. Bonds prices, however, also fluctuate with the length of the loan (the bond's maturity), with changes in the credit quality of the issuer, and with the general level of interest rates. Bond prices may be affected by supply and demand to a certain extent, but not to the same degree as stock.

Changes in interest rates have the greatest effect on bond prices. When interest rates increase, the prices of existing bonds drop, and conversely, when interest rates drop, the prices of existing bonds increase. Think of bond prices and interest rates sitting on opposite ends of a teeter-totter or seesaw. They are related but move in opposite directions. Imagine you own a 5% bond issued by Microsoft maturing twenty years from now. Since that bond was issued, interest rates in general have fallen. What would your friend pay to buy that bond now? More, or less, than you paid? More. If current rates are lower, a bond paying 5% is now more valuable. Its price increased.

When a company, Walmart, for example, issues a new bond, the rate of interest will be set. That rate depends on what interest rates other comparable companies are paying. To entice you to buy their new issue, Walmart must pay you a fair market rate; they must be competitive. One factor that affects the rate is the length of the loan: ten years, fifteen years, or twenty years, for example. You, the investor, would expect to be paid more to tie up your money for a longer period of time. Recently, there has not been much difference in short-term and long-term bond rates, however. Interest rates in general have been historically low.

Another factor affecting the rate of interest paid by a bond issuer is the issuer's credit quality. How likely is it that Walmart will pay you back? To help with the question about credit quality, there are independent companies, such as *Moody's, S&P Global Ratings, and Fitch Ratings,* which review the credit quality of potential borrowers. They rate the credit quality on a scale.

A credit rating for a bond is like your personal credit rating and, just like your personal credit rating, a company's credit rating can change over time. If your credit rating is low (because you are consistently late with payments, for example), you will typically be charged a higher percentage rate on your credit card debt. But by making regular payments over time and reducing your balance, your personal credit rating can be brought up, and you may then pay a lower rate of interest. Remember, for bonds, the credit quality is an indication of the likelihood that you will be repaid your principal, sometimes even interest. It is a measure of risk.

The highest credit quality bonds are AAA. The debt of the U.S. Treasury is rated AAA, for example. A chart of Moody's, S&P, and Fitch bond rating categories is included in the Glossary under "credit quality." Bonds with the ratings labeled *"investment grade"* are appropriate for a basic investment outfit.

WHAT KIND OF RETURN CAN I EXPECT FROM BONDS?

How about the total return of bonds? Because they hold less risk than stock, you would expect a lower return, which is generally true, but the return of bonds also fluctuates. From 1926 through 2009, bonds produced an average annual return of 5.8%, while stock produced an average annual return of 11.8%.[15] "As of June 11, 2020, the S&P 500 has a 10 year average annual return of 10.65%, while the U.S. bond market, measured by the Bloomberg Barclays U.S. Aggregate Bond Index, has a 10 year total return of 3.92%."[16] However, over the twenty years since 2000, although not uniformly, certain bonds outperformed stock.[17] Bond performance greatly depends on the general level and stability of interest rates, and current interest rates are at historic lows. No matter if the return from bonds is higher, lower, or the same as stock, bonds provide **diversification** and **lower the overall volatility** of your investment outfit, which adds value.

WHAT IS A MUNICIPAL BOND?

Some investors, those whose income puts them in the higher tax brackets, should consider mutual funds or ETFs containing bonds issued by municipalities—states, counties, cities, school districts, etc.—for the tax advantage they offer. The interest received from *municipal bonds* is generally not taxable at the federal level. It may also be state tax-exempt, especially if you reside in the same state as the municipality. The features of municipal bonds are like those of other bonds, but because of the tax benefit, they typically are issued with lower interest rates than *corporate bonds* with the same maturity and credit quality. The author suggests further study and/or the assistance of an investment advisor if you are interested and want to know more about municipal bonds.

Many factors affect the price of both stock and bonds, just as many factors affect the price of clothes. This primer covers the basics. In the same way that a cute blouse and a pair of jeans serve different purposes in an outfit, stocks and bonds serve different purposes. The unique characteristics of stocks and bonds complement each other and combined, offer diversification, which reduces risk. Your choices will reflect your style.

REVIEW

1. What do pants and skirts represent in an investment portfolio, and why?

2. What kind of return can you expect from investment grade U.S. bonds?

3. What factors affect the return of bonds?

4. Why do most investment outfits contain both stock and bonds?

CHAPTER FIFTEEN:

MIX AND MATCH

ARE YOU A MIX-AND-MATCH KIND OF PERSON? Do you like to put different pieces together to suit your personality? How can you show your style? You can find many, many choices of clothes to complete your outfit. It would be overwhelming, even impossible, to consider them all. So, where do you start? Start with your shoe choice, the allocation that the risk profile suggested—for example, 60% stock and 40% bonds. Review Chapter Four and Chapter Twelve, if needed.

PICK A TOP

Are you excited? It is time to shop for a blouse, shirt, or T-shirt for your basic outfit. Using a 60/40 stock-to-bond mix, select a stock mutual fund or ETF that will comprise 60% of your outfit.

There are so many choices. You could choose a U.S. total stock market mutual fund or ETF and be done—long-sleeved blouse or shirt. A total U.S. stock market mutual fund or ETF would include stock of all sizes of companies: large, mid-size, and small. (In reality, the fund can't possibly hold shares of every U.S. publicly traded company. The manager chooses stocks to represent each segment. That is the same with a total bond market mutual fund.)

However, instead of a total stock market fund, another option is to layer. For example, you might choose to start with a U.S. large company stock mutual fund or ETF. Why? Large companies usually have been in existence for a long time, information about them is readily available, earnings are relatively stable from year to year, and they are more likely to pay investors a stock dividend. The operating expenses of a large company fund or ETF are likely to be low as well. Think of the large company part of the total stock market as a short-sleeved blouse or a T-shirt.

Then add another layer. To your T-shirt or blouse, add a sweater—a small company stock fund. Why add small companies? Small companies are typically newer to the scene, and they may be putting all their effort into growth or research, so they are less likely to pay a stock dividend. It may be more difficult to obtain general information and financial information about the company. By now, you should recognize that a lack of information means more risk, and when you accept more risk, you expect a greater return on your investment.

If you choose to layer and you own a large company stock fund and a small company stock fund, then perhaps add a mid-size company stock fund next. A mid-size company fund will have some characteristics of both large and small company funds.

EXAMPLES OF TOPS FOR A BASIC INVESTMENT OUTFIT:

- Total Stock Market/Broad Market/Russell 3000 Index Funds or ETFs

- S&P 500 Index/Russell 1000 Index Funds or ETFs

- U.S. Large Cap (Company) Funds or ETFs

- S&P 600 Index/Russell 2000 Index Funds or ETFs

- U.S. Small Cap (Company) Funds or ETFs

PICK A BOTTOM

The skirt or pants/jeans are the bond portion of your outfit, but which kind of bond mutual fund or ETF will you choose? You could choose a conservative, ankle-length skirt or a pair of pants, a total U.S. bond market mutual fund or ETF, for example. The bonds in that fund/ETF are representative of the entire investment grade taxable bond market: U.S. Treasuries, government agencies, mortgage-backed securities, and corporate bonds.

Or you might choose a bond fund with just U.S. Treasury securities and government agency securities. Although U.S. Treasuries are the highest credit quality debt available, they comprise only part of the total bond market—the most conservative part, such as a mid-calf length skirt or capris. An investment grade corporate bond fund or ETF has thousands of bonds from which to draw with varying credit quality, but they are also a subset of the bond universe and higher risk than U.S. Treasuries. They are comparable to a knee-length skirt or long shorts. A *high yield*/junk bond fund carries the greatest risk, so it might be comparable to a miniskirt or short shorts, and as indicated before, they are not appropriate for a basic outfit.

How much coverage do you want? Remember, the shorter the skirt, the greater the risk and the more volatility you may expect. One purpose of having bonds in your portfolio is to reduce risk and volatility. If you use a 60/40 asset allocation, the bond portion will comprise 40% of your outfit.

EXAMPLES OF BOTTOMS FOR A BASIC INVESTMENT OUTFIT:

- Total or Aggregate Bond Market Index Funds or ETF

- U.S. Treasury Bond Fund or ETF (may be broken into short-term, intermediate, and long-term bonds)

- U.S. Government Securities Fund or ETF

- Corporate Bond Fund or ETF (may be broken into short-term, intermediate, and long-term bonds)

Mutual funds and ETFs are available with both active and passive management. Do you recall our discussion in Chapter Nine about actively managed mutual funds and ETFs versus index mutual funds and ETFs? The bond and stock choices listed here are a mix: some index choices and some actively managed choices.

If you have forgotten the differences, review Chapter Nine and the pros and cons of each.

If you like lots of choices, choose the mix-and-match style of separate tops and bottoms. The sample stock and bond funds and ETFs listed are like the window display of your favorite clothing store–they show only a part of what is available. Use the mutual fund or ETF screeners available on financial websites to limit your selection. It will become easier as you gain experience. However, if you want to start with something simpler, then keep reading.

REVIEW

1. What is the investment equivalent of a shirt or blouse?

2. What style top do you choose? Pick one or two.

3. What is the investment equivalent of pants or a skirt?

4. What style bottoms do you choose? Pick one or two.

CHAPTER SIXTEEN:

ONE AND DONE

WHAT ABOUT A DRESS? Think of a dress as a combination of a shirt and a skirt in one mutual fund or ETF. The purpose of a dress is to make it easy to match a particular asset allocation or mix of stock and bonds. If needed, review the discussion of asset allocation in Chapter Four and Chapter Twelve.

ASSET ALLOCATION MUTUAL FUNDS

There are two varieties of dresses, or *asset allocation mutual funds*, and they might make your life easier. One keeps a relatively constant stock-to-bond mix: for example, 70% stock and 30% bonds. Those are called *balanced mutual funds*. The other type changes the allocation to add more bonds and reduce stock as you grow closer to the need for money, such as for higher education or retirement. The latter are called *target date mutual funds*. Both are common options in company retirement plans.

BALANCED MUTUAL FUNDS

Imagine you buy a balanced asset allocation mutual fund that targets 70% stock and 30% bonds. After your purchase, the price of stocks in general moves higher while bond prices stay the same. Due to the *appreciation* of the price of stock, over time, that portfolio will have more than 70% in stock and less than 30% in bonds. When that happens, the manager might sell stock, buy bonds, or do both to *rebalance* the mix to stay roughly 70/30. The fund's purpose, in this case, to provide a mix of 70% stock and 30% bonds, is a key driver of changes to the portfolio. The reallocation that takes place is like retailoring your favorite dress when you lose weight. You don't get rid of the dress; you have it "taken in."

The manager of a balanced asset allocation mutual fund could select stocks and bonds to compose the portfolio, but she might prefer index or actively managed mutual funds or ETFs. If she uses other mutual funds, it is called a *fund of funds* (her fund contains other mutual funds). In any case, you will get a diversity of stock and bonds and with just one investment—one beautiful dress.

Some balanced allocation mutual funds have names that sound like risk tolerance descriptions: conservative, moderate, or aggressive. Some may just be called "balanced," and it is up to you to research the allocation of stocks and bonds.

TARGET DATE MUTUAL FUNDS

In addition to balanced funds, there are also mutual funds that target a specific date when you will need your money—the year you enter college, for example. Issuers of this type of mutual fund usually offer target dates in five-year increments: 2025, 2030, 2035, 2040, etc. These funds also mix stocks and bonds. The further into the future a target date may be, the more stock she will typically put in the portfolio to get a higher potential return. Gradually, as the target date gets closer and closer, she will decrease the amount of stock and add more bonds and cash. Why? Because as you get closer to your retirement date or the date you will enter college or tech school, you want less volatility, plus you also need liquidity. You are counting on your investment to pay for retirement or education expenses. Think of it this way: when you are young, you may be comfortable with more risk, so you wear a short dress (more stock), but as you age, a dress with a longer hemline is usually more appropriate (more bonds).

For most people, retirement lasts many more years than college, and therefore the need for money from your investment outfit lasts longer. To ensure that you have enough money to last your lifetime, you want your investments to continue to grow. It makes sense to continue to hold stock in your portfolio even after you reach your retirement date. Otherwise, inflation will reduce your *purchasing power*. The percentage to keep in stock depends on how much income you need from your investment clothes in addition to other sources of income you may have, such as social security and pensions, and what other financial resources you have in addition to your investments. Recent research supports a need for a higher allocation to stock longer into retirement, especially with lengthening lifespans.

A one-and-done option is a good starting point for a new investor. If you do not want to spend time reviewing possible investment choices or have a limited amount of money to invest, this would be an easy way to get started and have a complete outfit. You could base your choice on the target date that you will need your money, or you could match your risk tolerance—your shoes. There are fewer decisions and, just like a dress, with one purchase, you have a complete outfit.

REVIEW

1. Describe the features of an asset allocation mutual fund.

2. Describe the features of a balanced asset allocation mutual fund.

3. Describe the features of a target date asset allocation mutual fund.

4. Why is it important to keep stock in an investment portfolio throughout retirement?

CHAPTER SEVENTEEN:

ACCESSORIES

YOUR BASIC OUTFIT—foundation, a skirt and blouse, or a dress—is now complete. You can certainly leave it at that and be done shopping. However, as you become more comfortable with investing and your investment portfolio grows, you might want to add some accessories. In the fashion world, accessories make a statement. Each accessory you add to your outfit sets you apart. What are accessories in the world of investments? There are so many options from which to choose. Where do you start?

A PURSE, ANYONE?

What woman would leave her house for any length of time without her wallet or purse? A purse is a logical addition to an investment outfit, and that role is comparable to international investments, both stocks and bonds. Why? The United States is a small part of the world's population (4–5%)[18] and roughly a quarter of the global economy.[19] To benefit from growth in the rest of the world, doesn't it make sense to invest there, too? If you do not, you will be missing out on roughly half of the worldwide investing opportunities. Also, when assets are bought and sold in foreign currencies, you benefit when that currency appreciates against the U.S. dollar. It is a *hedge* against the U.S. dollar. A hedge attempts to limit the downside risk. Of course, currency exchange rates could also move against you, and that is called *currency risk.*

There are stock mutual funds and ETFs that contain only international stocks from *developed markets*: Canada, Australia, and Western Europe, for example. Other riskier international stock mutual funds and ETFs contain stocks from *emerging markets*, stocks from countries moving toward an open market economy: Brazil, Russia, India, and China, for example. The additional risk comes from more unknowns and uncertainties and sometimes more economic and political instabilities.

You can also find mutual funds and ETFs that contain stocks or bonds from all over the world—*global funds*. Those will include some domestic (U.S.) choices as well as foreign choices. Or you might choose just international choices but from developed and emerging markets combined.

Just as with stock, some international bond funds specialize in developed market or emerging market debt, and others include bonds from around the world. International bond funds can even contain the debt of governments of foreign countries, *sovereign debt*. Some bond fund managers choose to hedge the currency risk of foreign bonds, and some do not.

HOW ABOUT A BELT?

Not every outfit needs a belt, and not every investment portfolio needs real estate. You may already invest in real estate through home ownership. Some factors that affect the price of real estate are different than stocks and bonds, and some are the same, so real estate adds further diversification.

You might choose to invest in real estate through a *real estate investment trust* (REIT), a company that owns, and usually operates, income-producing real estate. The properties held by a REIT could be shopping malls, office buildings, or hospitals, among others. Each of those types of property has its own cycle and associated risk. The REIT trust structure is like a mutual fund in that it owns many properties; however, REITs trade like ETFs in the stock market.

Mortgage-backed securities are another type of real estate-related investment. Do you or your parents have a mortgage on your house? A lender may sell your mortgage to someone who buys a whole group of mortgages and then packages similar mortgages into a security. A mortgage-backed securities package can be sold separately in the market, or it can be combined with many other packages in a mutual fund.

What all of these bring to your outfit is diversification—they both enhance and individualize the look of your outfit but do not dominate it.

A LITTLE BLING!

Want to add some jewelry? If you need income, high dividend-paying stock mutual funds, such as utility funds or ETFs, are a possibility. Or you might want to add a technology mutual fund or ETF, or a health care mutual fund or ETF. If you are into clothes, you might want to add a mutual fund or ETF investing in companies that will benefit from discretionary spending, like retail clothing stores.

If taking care of the environment is valuable to you, you might want to add a mutual fund or ETF that focuses on companies that are friendly to our planet. There are mutual fund managers who look for companies with a positive impact on the environment or companies with strong social and corporate governance (ESG) principles, along with positive financial performance.

You might have a burning desire to buy the stock of a particular company, such as Starbucks or Home Depot or Amazon. If you have a passion, there is probably a way for you to invest and support that passion. Are camping and hiking your thing? Cars? Designer clothes? Travel? Music? Movies? Gardening? The price of a single share of stock varies wildly. If your resources are limited and you would like to invest in stock, Charles Schwab recently introduced Schwab Stock Slices, which are fractional shares in any one of the S&P 500 companies. You can buy a single slice or up to ten slices in a single transaction for as little as five dollars each.

Have fun with this but remember: your basic outfit always comes first and should compose the bulk of your portfolio. Keep in mind that the accessories you choose must be incorporated into the overall allocation of stocks and bonds, and they should not overwhelm their respective allocation. If your allocation is 60% stock and 40% bonds, that should not change. An outfit made entirely of accessories would look pretty silly.

YOU ARE NOW DRESSED, AND YOU LOOK GORGEOUS!

REVIEW

1. What does a purse represent in an investment outfit?

2. What does a belt represent in an investment outfit?

3. What accessories do you want to add to your outfit?

4. How do your accessories affect your overall portfolio allocation?

5. How will the addition of the accessories change the risk and return profile of your portfolio?

6. **Build four sample outfits**. Assume that you have already set aside six months of fixed expenses as your emergency fund or foundation. **You have $30,000 left to invest.** As you make your selections, pay attention to expenses. The lower the OER, the better. Make your outfit very basic, and use the following as a guide:

Shoes = Asset Allocation. Use the mix of stocks and bonds suggested by your risk tolerance assessment, or if you prefer, use 80/20 for this exercise. (Examples use an 80/20 allocation.)

OUTFIT #1 = A DRESS

Select a balanced fund that matches your shoes. Start with an online search. For example, search for "80/20 mutual fund" and then compare the returns and expenses of the funds that are listed. If you opened a brokerage account/ closet, you could also use the brokerage firm's website to do your research.

Example: ABC 80/20 Target Allocation Fund $30,000

Your choice:

OUTFIT #2 = A MIX-AND-MATCH OUTFIT

Top = One stock mutual fund or ETF

Bottom = One bond mutual fund or ETF

Example:	Total U.S. Stock Market Index Fund/ETF	$24,000
	Total U.S. Bond Market Index Fund/ETF	$6,000

Your choices:

OUTFIT #3 = ANOTHER MIX-AND-MATCH OUTFIT

Top = Two stock mutual funds or ETFs

Bottom = Two bond mutual funds or ETFs

Example:	S&P 500 Index Fund/ETF	$16,000
	Small Company Mutual Fund/ETF	$8,000
	Total U.S. Bond Market Index Fund/ETF	$4,000
	Intermediate Corporate Bond Fund/ETF	$2,000

Your choices:

OUTFIT #4 = ADD A PURSE (EITHER A STOCK OR BOND PURSE) AND AN ACCESSORY TO OUTFIT #2

Example:　Total U.S. Stock Market
Index Fund/ETF　　　　　　　　　　$20,000

International Developed Markets
Stock Fund/ETF　　　　　　　　　　$3,000

Stock of XYZ Company　　　　　　　$1,000

Total U.S. Bond
Market Index Fund/ETF　　　　　　　$6,000

Your choices:

THOSE ARE ALL BASIC INVESTMENT OUTFITS.

PART FOUR

Congratulations! You now know how to put together a fabulous outfit combining stocks and bonds using mutual funds and ETFs. Well done! I knew you could do it.

Are you wondering in which closet to hang that new outfit? There are lots of choices of closets, and some make more sense in certain situations than others. Sometimes a closet will be chosen for you. For example, your employer will likely choose a closet for your company retirement plan. In other cases, you will be able to choose.

CHAPTER EIGHTEEN:

MORE ABOUT CLOSETS

WHETHER YOU ARE PURCHASING clothes for saving or investing, your account/closet will have a name or title. The name identifies the owner of the closet and, in some cases, why you are investing. It may also name a beneficiary. Your closet is where you hang your clothes (your investments), and it tells everyone to whom the clothes belong. Although it is a good idea to keep your saving clothes and your investing clothes in different closets, the closets may have the same name—individual account, for example.

It is important to remember that tax consequences are associated with the closets that you choose. Income, dividends, and capital gains are taxed (usually annually) when clothes are held in a taxable account/closet. On the other hand, taxes may not be due until funds are permanently removed (a distribution is taken) from a tax-advantaged account/closet. (Sometimes no tax is due. For example, certain distributions from a Roth IRA or a 529 College Savings Plan may not be taxed.) Taxes, like fees and expenses, reduce your investment return, so pay attention to them.

It makes sense to put short-term savings in taxable closets because money can move in and out of the closet with fewer, if any, penalties. Tax-advantaged closets are meant for long-term investing, such as for retirement and education. However, all tax-advantaged closets have restrictions on who is eligible to make contributions and limits on how much can be added to them annually. After you have maximized what you can put in tax-advantaged closets, you may want to make long-term investments in a taxable closet as well.

The following are examples, first of taxable closets and then tax-advantaged closets:

TAXABLE

Tax is usually due each year on any income: interest, dividends, and capital gains (profit on securities you have sold).

- **Individual Account:** A closet owned by a single person.

- *Joint Account:* A closet owned by two or more people.

- *Custodial UGMA or UTMA Account:* A closet owned by a minor but managed by an adult custodian whose name also appears on the account. Upon reaching the *age of majority,* the age at which a child legally becomes an adult, the closet name is changed to the minor's name alone. Federal *gift tax* rules apply to contributions. (A donor is assessed and must pay a gift tax if the gift is over a certain dollar limit.)

- **Trust Account:** A closet owned by a *trust*: a legal entity created to hold assets for the benefit of another.

- **Corporate or Business Account:** A closet owned by a company or business: a corporation, a limited liability company, or a partnership, for example.

TAX-ADVANTAGED (THESE CLOSETS HAVE ANNUAL CONTRIBUTION LIMITS)

No tax is due on any income or the appreciation of assets until funds are removed permanently from the account/closet. In some cases, no tax is due at all.

Individual Retirement Account/Arrangement (IRA): A closet owned by an individual whose purpose is to invest for retirement. Employed persons and non-employed spouses may establish an IRA as long as the household has earned income equal to or greater than the contribution. Subsets of IRAs are:

- Traditional IRAs: Investment contributions **may** be tax-deductible.

- Roth IRAs: Investment contributions are **not** tax-deductible, are made with after-tax money (money that has already been taxed, such as a paycheck), and therefore distributions are usually not taxed; however, specific rules must be met.

- Rollover IRAs—Traditional or Roth: Receives a transfer of funds from a company retirement plan such as a 401(k). A rollover usually occurs at either retirement or end of service.

Defined-Contribution Company Retirement Plans: A plan an employer offers as a benefit to employees, in which part of the employee's income may be deferred to invest for retirement. Employee contributions are usually deducted from each paycheck, and sometimes the employer will match employee contributions up to a certain percentage. In other cases, the employer makes the entire contribution. Rules for distributions to be tax-free vary with the type of plan and are contained in the plan document. Investments are self-directed, which means each employee selects her own investments. Examples:

- 401(k) (pre-tax contributions) or Roth 401(k) (after-tax contributions)

- 403(b) (pre-tax contributions) or Roth 403(b) (after-tax contributions): Used by public education, nonprofits, and some ministers

- 457 (pre-tax contributions) or Roth 457 (after-tax contributions): Offered by state and local governments, employee contributions only

- SEP IRAs (pre-tax contributions): Used by some self-employed individuals and offered by some small businesses, employer contributions only

- SIMPLE IRAs (pre-tax contributions): Offered by some small businesses

Defined-Benefit Pension Plans: A plan an employer offers as a benefit to employees, in which payments to retired employees are based on a formula that takes into account the employee's earnings history, years of service, and age, rather than payments made based on contributions and investment returns. In this type of plan, professional managers make investment choices on behalf of the company and its employees.

Education Savings Accounts: A closet housing funds intended to cover expenses of education for a specific individual, the account beneficiary. The account/closet owner, who may be the same person as the beneficiary but usually is not, chooses investments and makes account changes. Closet owners may be parents or grandparents, for example. Federal gift tax rules apply to contributions. (A donor is assessed and must pay a gift tax if the gift is over a certain dollar limit.) When money is taken out of the account/closet, the earned income portion of the withdrawal may not be taxed if the funds are used for specific education-related purposes.

- 529 College Savings Plan (after-tax contributions): Used to cover qualified education expenses from kindergarten through graduate school. All fifty states offer College Savings Plans. Accounts/closets are administered by each state; therefore, rules on contributions and the investment choices vary from state to state. You may invest in any state's plan.

- *529 ABLE Accounts* (after-tax contributions): Like a 529 college savings plan, 529 ABLE closets are savings accounts/closets administered by the states. Money can be withdrawn tax-free when the funds are used to pay for qualified disability expenses.

- *Coverdell Education Savings Account* (after-tax contributions): Used to cover both qualified K–12 and higher education expenses. Beneficiaries must be eighteen years of age or younger when the account is established, and funds must be used by age thirty. High-income individuals may not be able to contribute to this type of closet per legislative restriction. The annual maximum contribution is $2,000 per beneficiary from all sources.

The list of closets or account types is not all-encompassing; however, those listed are the most common. Each comes with different features. Some closets are big, and some are smaller and more specialized. **Please refer to the account or plan documents for further definitions, pertinent rules, and regulations.**

REVIEW

1. What is the difference between a taxable and a tax-advantaged closet?

2. What type of closets could you use to save for college or technical school? Name two and describe their differences.

3. What type of closet could you use to save for retirement? Describe one that is sponsored by a company and one that you could open as an individual.

CHAPTER NINETEEN:

DO I WANT HELP?

IF YOU DECIDE THAT YOU WANT HELP and have the financial resources to pay, you might want to hire an advisor. An advisor is like a personal shopper whose services may be offered by a store, or she may be totally independent. In the investment world, an advisor may be employed by a brokerage firm, a bank or credit union, or a mutual fund company, for example. She may also be independent of any of those, in business for herself or for some-one else.

What an *investment advisor* will charge for her services varies but is usually expressed as a percentage of the assets, the market value of the investments, that she manages for you. It could be 1% annually, or lower, or higher. Ask. This fee will be in addition to any clothes-related charges. It is the cost of her advice. You pay for the clothes a personal shopper selects, plus you pay for her service. Most advisors require a certain level of assets to qualify for their service. That amount could be $500,000 or even $1 million but can often be a combination of all your accounts/closets. For example, a $600,000 IRA; $350,000 trust; and $50,000 college saving plan would meet a $1 million requirement.

HOW DO I CHOOSE AN ADVISOR?

If you choose to use an advisor, it is important to find someone you trust and someone who is a FIDUCIARY. A fiduciary is bound legally and ethically to put your interests first. That is not a universal requirement in the industry. For example, as of June 30, 2020, employees of brokerage firms are held to a BEST INTEREST requirement. The U.S. Securities and Exchange Commission (SEC), which holds primary responsibility for enforcing federal securities laws, wanted to make it clear that a broker-dealer may not put (her own) financial interests ahead of the interests of a retail customer when making recommendations.[20] She must make choices based on the "Best Interest" of her client.

What, then, is the difference between a broker-dealer exercising "Best Interest" and a fiduciary? Being a fiduciary is the highest legal duty of one party to another. It is a higher standard of care. How do you find an advisor who is a fiduciary? Look for a *Registered Investment Advisor* (RIA) or a CERTIFIED FINANCIAL PLANNER™ professional. You can search for an advisor in your area who is a CFP® professional at the following website: **letsmakeaplan.org**.

A good place to find information about a particular firm, both broker-dealer and SEC-registered RIA, is to ask for the firm's Form CRS, which is a summary of the firm's services and fees. It contains descriptions of the types of preferred customers (individuals, institutions, retirement plans, etc.), services offered, fees and costs, conflicts of interest (for example, if they receive a personal benefit by choosing a certain product over another, **pay close attention**), Standard of Conduct (how are employees expected to act), disciplinary history (**also pay close attention to this**), as well as other information. Form CRS is written in understandable language, and its purpose is to help you decide if you want to work with a particular advisory firm.

In addition, advisors, whether licensed by a state or the SEC, are required to file a Form ADV Parts 1 and 2 through the Investment Advisor Registration Depository (IARD) operated by FINRA. Applicants for registration as an investment advisor representative must file a Form U4. The public may access that information online at **adviserinfo.sec.gov**. The North American Securities Administrators Association (NASAA) website, **nasaa. org**, provides a link to "Contact Your Regulator" for access to individual state websites.

As you interview individual advisors, the following questions may be helpful:[21]

1. What are your qualifications and credentials?

2. What services do you offer?

3. Will you have a **fiduciary** duty to me?

4. What is your approach to financial planning/investing?

5. What types of clients do you serve?

6. Will you be the only advisor working with me?

7. How will I pay?

8. How much do you charge?

9. Do others stand to gain from the financial advice you give me?

10. Have you ever been publicly disciplined for unlawful or unethical actions in your career?

Before you select a particular advisor, it is also a good idea to check her background, work history, and any client complaints. There are two sources for that information. If the advisor is associated with a broker-dealer, use FINRA's BrokerCheck: **brokercheck.finra.org**. If the advisor is associated with a Registered Investment Advisor, then use the SEC website: **sec.gov/check-your-investment-professional**.

If you choose an independent advisor, a RIA, it is also important to ask, "Where will my assets/clothes be held?" A Registered Investment Advisor should not mix your clothes with other clients' clothes. They should create separate closets and use a third-party custodian, such as Pershing, Schwab, or Fidelity, to hold the clothes. When there is a third-party custodian, you can expect to receive two statements: one from your advisor and a separate one from the custodian. The two should reflect the same information.

The statements from the custodian should clearly show that you are the owner of the account/closet.

Why is a separate custodian important? Unfortunately, there have been instances of advisors mixing funds from client closets and then using the funds for themselves. An unethical advisor may create her own client statements with false information, and if there is no custodian statement for comparison, the situation could go undetected.

EXAMPLES OF ADVISORY ARRANGEMENTS

Advisory relationships and the compensation methods associated with them vary. Every year advisors find new ways to market their advice and make it more affordable. That is a good thing! Currently, the following arrangements are the most common.

INDEPENDENT REGISTERED INVESTMENT ADVISORS

You recently met with Susie Smith, who owns Susie Smith Investment Management Company, a Registered Investment Advisor (RIA). You decided to meet with Susie upon the recommendation of a good friend and after reviewing the information on her website. After talking with Susie and reviewing the ten questions listed earlier, you find that she acts as a fiduciary, her fees are reasonable, and she clearly understands your goals, which are reflected in the strategy she suggests. You are comfortable asking Susie questions, she is patient and thorough with her responses, and she answers in language you understand. After going through the same process with two other potential advisor candidates—one intimidates you and keeps interrupting (run!), and the other does not talk in language you understand—you decide to hire Susie to manage your portfolio.

The securities Susie selects will be held at a brokerage firm, let's say Fidelity (the custodian), for safekeeping. The account/closet will clearly state the owner in its title. You will receive statements from both Susie Smith Investment Management and Fidelity. Check to see that the two statements reflect the same purchases and sales and the same fees. If the two statements are issued on the same day, the market values of your investments should match as well. Susie's service is similar to an independent personal shopper.

BROKER-DEALER ADVISORS

Before forming her own firm, Susie was employed by TD Ameritrade. TD Ameritrade is a brokerage firm. All the investments she chose for her clients while working at TD Ameritrade were held at TD Ameritrade, and her clients received regular statements that included the purchases and sales she made and the market value of those investments. The statement came directly from TD Ameritrade. Susie did not issue separate statements. Susie's service, using the shopping comparison, is offered by a store, a broker-dealer. There may be a separate charge for her expertise, or it may be included as part of the services offered by the store.

Susie's compensation at TD Ameritrade and at Susie Smith Investment Management is likely different. Ask. An advisor may be paid based on the assets she manages for you, with a monthly or quarterly retainer, or by an hourly or flat fee. She may also receive commissions on the products/clothes you buy. Always go through the questions listed earlier. **Above all else, make sure the person that you hire acts as a fiduciary.**

ROBO-ADVISORS

Midway between hiring a financial advisor and doing it your-self are *robo-advisors*. A relatively new addition to the advisor scene, this option is especially suitable for beginning investors. Robo-advisors provide financial advice and investment manage-ment **online** with moderate to minimal human interaction. The digital financial advice is based on mathematical rules. Software automatically selects, allocates, and then manages client assets. Accounts/closets can typically be opened with as little as $100, some with no minimum, but then you may pay a monthly fee to cover costs.

Robo-advisor type closets are offered at the major brokerage firms such as Fidelity, Schwab, and Vanguard. However, you may be better off—lower fees, lower investment minimums, or better returns—at one of the independent robo-advisory firms such as Betterment, Wealthfront, or Ellevest (see **roboadvisorpros.com** for a robo-advisor guide). How do you compare returns? Do you remember the risk assessment that you completed in Chapter Four? If possible, use the suggested asset allocation from that exercise, 60% stock/40% bonds, for example, and either search online or ask about returns using that allocation. Compare fees, transaction charges, minimums, and any other restrictions. Make sure all your questions are answered.

At some point in your investment life, you may want the help of an advisor, a professional shopper. Please be careful and take time with your choice. You want that person to not only be professional, ethical, and knowledgeable but also understand your goals and your risk tolerance—know your style. It is important that they talk in language that you understand and are properly registered and licensed. Unless you use a robo-advisor, make sure your advisor acts as a **fiduciary**. Diligent research will make for a better match and a long-term relationship.

REVIEW

1. What does it mean to be a fiduciary? Why is it important?

2. How is a "Best Interest" standard different from a fiduciary standard?

3. How are an independent advisor (RIA) and an advisor at a brokerage firm different? How are they the same?

4. Why is it important to check your investment statements?

5. What is a robo-advisor? What is different about this advisor alternative?

CHAPTER TWENTY:

FINAL NOTES

FIRST, CONGRATULATE YOURSELF for the step you have taken to achieve your financial goals. You can learn a lot more if you are interested. The information included in this primer provides only the essentials.

WHAT IS MISSING?

Did you miss it? Nothing in this primer discussed or tried to select the next hot stock, ETF, or mutual fund or even predict in what direction the stock and bond markets might move. Hopefully, at this point, you will agree that it is not appropriate to try to pick a single or even a couple of winning stocks. Diversity is the key when you start to build a basic investment outfit. Likewise, an investor with a long-term goal will, with the right asset allocation and a healthy emergency fund, weather market upturns and downturns without flinching.

You may have also noticed that the mutual fund and ETF examples listed were generic. To find specific mutual funds or ETFs, use an online search engine (e.g., search for "low expense ratio U.S. stock ETFs"), or use FINRA's mutual fund database or a brokerage firm's research function. Many broker-dealers have information available to the general public.

After you select the ETFs or funds that you want to purchase, you may need their *trading symbol*, the unique series of letters (and sometimes numbers) assigned to a security for trading purposes. Every stock, ETF, and mutual fund has a trading symbol. Some bonds, those traded on exchanges, also have a trading symbol. Trading symbols can be easily found through an online search.

Also missing is any discussion of insurance companies (stores) and their products (clothes) that combine investing with life insurance. In some circumstances, such a piece of clothing may be appropriate for a beginning investor. There are different kinds of expenses and fees associated with life insurance, however, so please consult with an advisor who is a fiduciary before you make that decision.

A discussion of trust companies or trust departments of banks is also missing. Such entities serve in a fiduciary role as trustee to administer trusts—distribute funds and property according to the specifications of the trust—and to invest trust assets according to the trust document. Those services are offered for a fee. Unless you are a beneficiary of a trust, or your family circumstances warrant creation of a trust, a beginning investor is not likely to use the services of a trust company or department.

WANT TO LEARN MORE?

If you are interested in broader financial topics, the following list provides a starting point:

- Cash Flow Planning

- Debt Management

- Education Planning

- Investment Planning

- Retirement Saving and Income Planning

- Tax Planning

- Risk Management and Insurance Planning

- Estate Planning

All of these are interrelated and are part of a comprehensive financial plan. Resources are plentiful. Look for classes in your community, books, or online references. Some nonprofit organizations, such as the Financial Planning Association, offer educational resources. The Financial Industry Regulatory Authority (FINRA), which regulates broker-dealers, has a fund analyzer. The FDIC, through its Money Smart program, is another resource for information on financial topics. In some areas of the U.S., the YWCA offers a financial literacy seminar series for women in cooperation with MoneyW!SE. Check with your local YWCA for availability and qualifications. Military OneSource has online financial resources and tools available to service families.

Although only 26% of people aged thirteen to twenty-one say their parents taught them how to manage money, I am encouraged that, as of July 2019, twenty states require a financial literacy class for students in high school. It is my sincere hope that one day personal finance instruction, including the investment basics offered in this primer, will be **required** at some level of education nationwide.

NEXT STEPS

Imagine this: a friend just moved to a new house in a big city. She asked you to come to her house-warming party, and you accepted. With gift in hand, you get in your car and set the GPS to her new address. Will you get there? It may be difficult. You must do something additional: start the car's engine, back out of the driveway, and enter the road. Setting the goal does absolutely no good unless you take additional steps, sometimes lots of them. You may encounter a detour or make a wrong turn along your journey, and then the GPS will recalibrate. No problem. If you are diligent and keep your eye on the goal, you will eventually arrive at your destination.

It's the same with saving and investing. It is not enough to set goals; you must do something else—open an account, deposit money, choose investments, and monitor your progress. Life may throw you a curve that may require you to change goals, or you may decide to take a totally different route. Recalibrate and keep going. Stay the course, and you will succeed. I know it!

ACKNOWLEDGMENTS

I AM INDEBTED TO MANY FRIENDS, relatives, and colleagues who took the time to read through my manuscript at various phases. Their edits, comments, and suggestions greatly enhanced the final product.

My thanks go to my sisters–Dorie, Betty, Shirley, and Bonnie–who edited the earliest version and provided support and encouragement throughout the process. Special hugs to Bonnie, who did a second review. My dear friend Carolyn McKenna offered a gut check midway through and gave me more ideas to think about. I am especially grateful to my colleagues Michelle Buonincontri, Lindsay Frazier Martinez, Barbara Boosman, and Kathleen Murray, who edited at various stages and detailed many ways to improve the message. Michelle two times! They not only offered suggestions of key concepts that should be included, most of which made the final version, but also ways to change the layout to increase readability.

I also want to thank C.J. Redwine with kn literary arts and Jennifer Jas of Words With Jas LLC for their professional editing.

They made this book not only more readable, but also brought new ideas to the table. I learned a lot about the mechanics of writing from these two ladies. Who knew there are three types of dashes? My deepest gratitude, however, goes to Camille Parker with My Word Publishing. Camille guided me step by step through the publishing industry maze. I had so much to learn, and this book would not be in print without her patient assistance! She is a true gem.

A huge shout-out goes to Britta Bowers and Julie Cook of Idea Three Creative. You made sense of my vision and brought it to life online in full color! Likewise, kudos to Victoria Wolf of Wolf Design and Marketing whose artistic talent is showcased in the book layout and cover designs.

The excitement of the women who attended my classes at Fresh Start Women's Foundation in Phoenix, not only to feed their desire to learn about investing but also to write this book, gave me confirmation of its need. The echo of their voices brought me through some inevitable disappointments and delays in the process to bring *How to Dress a Naked Portfolio* to market.

Finally, I owe a huge thank you to my partner, Jody. He tolerated my hours on the computer during the isolation demanded by COVID-19, along with the ups and downs of good and bad days of inspiration. His support, encouragement, and love allowed me to give birth to this book, which has been one of my life goals.

Thank you, one and all!

Bev Bowers

GLOSSARY

529 College Savings Plan/529 ABLE Accounts: 529 Plans are tax-advantaged accounts that are meant to be used to save to cover qualified education expenses from kindergarten through graduate school. 529 ABLE accounts are meant to be used to save to cover qualified disability expenses. 529 plans and accounts originate from states, not the federal government, so the rules differ from state to state.

Active Management: A person or team of people who use analytical research, forecasts, and their own judgment and experience to make investment decisions on what securities to buy, hold, and sell to maximize return.

Administrative Fee: Expenses charged to cover costs associated with opening, maintaining, changing, or closing an account.

Advisory Fee: Fee paid for professional advisory services on matters related to money, finances, and investments. The fee may be charged as a percentage of total assets on an ongoing basis, or it may be one-time only.

Age of Majority: The point in time when minors cease to be considered minors and assume legal control over their persons, actions, and decisions. The Age of Majority in most states is eighteen.

Appreciation: An increase in monetary value.

Asset (Financial): A liquid, non-physical asset whose value is derived from a contractual claim: bank balances, stocks, and bonds, for example.

Asset Allocation: An investment strategy that attempts to balance risk with reward by adjusting the percentage of each asset class (stocks, bonds, and cash equivalents) in the portfolio according to the investor's risk tolerance, goals, and investment time frame.

Asset Allocation Mutual Fund: A mutual fund that uses an asset allocation investment strategy. The portfolio mixes stocks, bonds, and cash equivalents to diversify the fund and avoid volatility in any one market to maximize return.

Asset Classes: A group of financial instruments, such as stock, which have similar financial characteristics, are subject to the same laws and regulations, and behave similarly in the marketplace.

Assets Under Management (AUM): Total market value of investments that a person or entity manages on behalf of clients.

Balanced Mutual Fund: A type of asset allocation mutual fund that maintains a more-or-less fixed ratio of stocks to bonds to balance growth and income.

Blue-Chip Stocks: Common stocks in corporations with a national reputation for quality, reliability, and the ability to operate profitably in good and bad times.

Bond: An instrument of indebtedness of the bond issuer to the bondholders. A bond obligates the issuer to pay the bondholder a specified sum of money, usually at specific intervals (interest), and to repay the principal amount of the loan at maturity. The most common types of bonds are U.S. Treasury, corporate, and municipal.

Bond Interest: The specified sum of money, usually at specific intervals, the issuer of a bond pays the bondholders. It is generally a percentage of the amount borrowed. See also Interest.

Bondholder: Owner of a bond who is entitled to interest payments as specified and the return of the principal when the bond matures.

Broker-Dealer or Brokerage Firm: A person or firm in the business of buying and selling securities for and from its own account (dealer) or on behalf of customers (broker). Broker-dealer licenses are granted by the SEC; however, broker-dealer firms and their registered brokers are regulated by FINRA.

Brokerage Account: An arrangement in which an investor deposits money (opens an account) with a licensed brokerage firm to place trades to buy and sell securities. The investor may initiate those trades online or through a licensed representative of the firm. The assets belong to the investor.

Budget: An estimation of income and expenses over a specified future period.

Capital Gain: The rise in value of an investment or real estate that gives it a higher worth than the adjusted purchase price. The gain is not established or realized until the asset is sold. The amount of a realized gain must be claimed for income tax.

Certificate of Deposit (CD): A debt instrument issued by a financial institution for a specific fixed term, usually with a fixed interest rate. CDs are commonly sold by banks, savings institutions, and credit unions.

CERTIFIED FINANCIAL PLANNER™/CFP® Certification: A professional designation conferred on candidates in the U.S. by the Certified Financial Planner Board of Standards. Along with a bachelor's degree, a candidate must meet requirements in four areas: specialized education, comprehensive exam, experience, and ethics. An annual fee is required to maintain certification as well as continuing education and adherence to the Code of Ethics and Standards of Conduct. A CFP® professional is committed to an expanded fiduciary duty–duty of loyalty, duty of care, and duty to follow client instructions.

Commercial Bank: A for-profit corporation with a charter issued at the local, state, or national level. Banks issue stock, which is owned by investors, and those investors elect a board of directors who oversee the bank's operations.

Commission: A fee paid to a broker for executing purchases and sales of securities for a customer.

Common Stock: Ownership of a company represented by shares that are a claim on earnings and assets. A single share of the stock represents fractional ownership of the corporation in proportion to the total number of shares.

Company Retirement Savings Plan: Employer-sponsored plans meant to encourage employees to automatically save for retirement. Some employers match employee contributions to the plan up to a certain level. There may be tax benefits for both the employee and employer.

Compounding: A process in which an asset's earnings, from either capital gains or interest, are reinvested to generate additional earnings over time.

Concentration Risk: The potential for loss in value to a portfolio when an individual or group of investments (from the same industry or sector, for example) move together in an unfavorable direction.

Corporate Account: Any account, brokerage, bank, etc., whose owner is a legal business entity such as a corporation or limited partnership.

Corporate Bond: A type of debt security issued by a corporation to raise funds for a variety of reasons: expansion, acquisitions, or ongoing operations, for example.

Coverdell Education Savings Account: A tax-advantaged investment account designed to encourage saving to cover future education expenses.

Credit Quality: One of the criteria for judging the investment quality of a bond or bond mutual fund. The bond rating is a measure of a bond issuer's ability to repay the debt and the risk of default.

Credit Union: A credit union is a state or federally chartered nonprofit savings and lending cooperative owned and controlled by its members. Credit union members are its account holders.

Currency Risk/Exchange-Rate Risk: The risk that a change in price of one currency in relation to another, the exchange rate, will negatively affect the profitability of an investment.

Custodial Fee: A fee a brokerage or other financial institution charges for safekeeping services. See Custodian.

Custodial UTMA/UGMA Account: An account set up for the benefit of a beneficiary, often a minor, administered by a legal guardian or custodian who has a fiduciary obligation to the beneficiary (Uniform Transfers to Minors Act or Uniform Gifts to Minors Act).

Custodian: An institution that holds securities for safekeeping on behalf of a client to reduce the risk of theft or loss.

Dealer: See Broker-Dealer.

Defined-Benefit Pension Plan: A company retirement plan set up to provide a specific payment to a retiree for the rest of their lifetime. The payment amount is calculated using a formula based on the employee's age, length of service, and salary at retirement.

Developed Market: A country with a more advanced economy, better-developed infrastructure, mature capital markets, and high standards of living. Examples are the United States, Canada, the United Kingdom, and the European Union.

Discretionary Expenses: Costs for nonessential items or services. Expenses a household can get by without, if necessary.

Diversification: A risk management strategy that mixes a wide variety of investments with different characteristics within a portfolio.

Dividend: A sum of money paid by a company to its shareholders out of its profits or reserves. See also Stock Dividend. Mutual funds are required by law to pass along any income they receive (interest from a bond or dividends from stock) to shareholders. This is also called a dividend distribution. Some ETFs also make dividend distributions.

Dollar Cost Averaging: An investment strategy of buying a fixed dollar amount of a specific investment at set intervals to limit the impact of price volatility.

Early Withdrawal Penalty (CD): A charge a financial institution assesses if funds are withdrawn from a fixed-term investment prior to maturity. Early withdrawal penalties vary by institution and by investment term.

Emergency Fund: A readily available source of money meant to improve financial security by creating a safety net that can be used to meet emergency expenses.

Emerging Market: A country or market that has some characteristics of a developed market but does not fully meet its standards. Examples are Brazil, Russia, India, and China.

Equity: Ownership interest possessed by shareholders in a company. A stockholder expects to share in the profits of a company and to benefit from its growth.

Estate: Assets a person possesses at the time of death.

Exchange: Central location where securities trading takes place.

Exchange Traded Fund (ETF): An investment fund, much like a mutual fund, that is traded on stock exchanges like stock. An ETF can hold stock, commodities, or bonds, for example.

Face Value/Par Value: The nominal value of a bond or stock. For a stock, par value is usually $1, which is not related to the stock's market value. The face value of a bond or CD is the basis to determine interest payments and, at the maturity date, is the value the holder receives if the issuer doesn't default.

Federal Deposit Insurance Corporation (FDIC): An independent agency created by Congress to maintain stability and public confidence in the nation's financial system. The agency insures deposits in banks and thrift institutions.

Fiduciary: A person or company who holds a legal or ethical relationship of good faith and trust with a beneficiary—a person, or group of people—putting the beneficiaries' interests ahead of their own. A fiduciary prudently takes care of money or other assets. A fiduciary could be a corporate trust company or department, a financial advisor or financial planner, or managers of pension plans and endowments. Fiduciaries are regulated under various statutes and laws.

Financial Industry Regulatory Authority (FINRA): An independent, non-governmental organization that writes and enforces the rules governing registered brokers and broker-dealer firms in the U.S.

Fixed Income Securities: A type of investment under which the borrower or issuer is obliged to make payments of a fixed amount on a fixed schedule.

Fixed or Non-Discretionary Expenses: Expenses that stay the same each month: rent or mortgage, car payments, car insurance, property taxes, home insurance, and school loans, for example.

Fund of Funds: A mutual fund portfolio consisting of other mutual funds rather than stocks, bonds, or other securities. They are sometimes called multi-manager funds.

Gift Tax: The tax assessed on money or property that one living person gives to another. Many gifts are not subject to taxation because of exemptions written in tax laws. The gift tax is levied on the giver, not the receiver.

Global Fund: A mutual fund of ETFs that can invest in securities throughout the world, including the United States.

Hedge: A strategy used to offset investment risk to protect against potential losses or gains.

High Yield Bond: A bond that is rated below investment grade. They carry a higher risk of default but offer higher returns than better quality bonds to compensate for that risk. Sometimes called a Junk Bond.

Income: Earnings that come from interest payments, dividends, capital gains, or any other profit made through an investment of any kind.

Independent Broker-Dealers: Firms that typically cater to more experienced advisors who generate high streams of revenue but who desire support for such things as compliance and trade execution.

Index: An index typically measures the performance of a basket of securities intended to mirror a certain part of the market. An index may also measure economic data, such as inflation.

Individual Account: A taxable account opened for, and owned by, one person.

Individual Retirement Account (IRA): A tax-advantaged account that employed individuals and their spouses use to invest for retirement.

Inflation: A sustained increase in the general price of goods and services over a period, which results in a fall in the purchasing value of money.

Interest: The cost of borrowing money for a certain period. It is generally a percentage of the amount borrowed. See also Bond Interest.

International Stock: Stock issued by corporations outside the United States. The stock may or may not be traded on a U.S. stock exchange.

Investment: Monetary asset purchased to provide income or to be sold later at a higher price for a profit.

Investment Advisor: A person or group that makes investment recommendations or conducts securities analysis for a fee.

Investment Company: A firm that, for a management fee, invests the pooled funds of investors in securities appropriate for its stated investment objective.

Investment Grade: Refers to the quality of a company's credit. To be considered an investment grade issue, the company must be rated BBB- or higher by S&P or Fitch, or Baa3 or higher by Moody's. The three primary credit rating agencies are Moody's, S&P Global Ratings, and Fitch Ratings (see chart).

	Moody's	S&P	Fitch	Meaning
Investment Grade bonds	Aaa	AAA	AAA	Prime
	Aa1	AA+	AA+	High grade
	Aa2	AA	AA	
	Aa3	AA-	AA-	
	A1	A+	A+	Upper medium grade
	A2	A	A	
	A3	A-	A-	
	Baa1	BBB+	BBB+	Lower medium grade
	Baa2	BBB	BBB	
	Baa3	BBB-	BBB-	
Junk bonds	Ba1	BB+	BB+	Non investment grade speculative
	Ba2	BB	BB	
	Ba3	BB-	BB-	
	B1	B+	B+	Highly speculative
	B2	B	B	
	B3	B-	B-	
	Caa1	CCC+	CCC+	Substantial risks
	Caa2	CCC	CCC	Extremely speculative
	Caa3	CCC-	CCC-	In default with unlikely prospect for recovery
	Ca	CC	CC+	
		C	CC	
			CC-	
	D	D	D	In default

Source: Hobbs, Jonathan (2017, June) Bond Investing Explained: Risk, Interest Rates, and Bond Prices. Retrieved from: https://www.stopsaving.com/investing in bonds/

Joint Account (Joint Tenants/Joint Tenants with Right of Survivorship/Tenants in Common/Community Property): An account opened in the name of two or more individuals or entities. Ownership rights vary with the type of joint ownership selected.

Junk Bond: A bond that is rated below investment grade. They carry a higher risk of default but offer higher returns than better-quality bonds to compensate for that risk.

Ladder: A strategy in which an investor divides a sum of money into pieces with different maturity dates.

Liquidity: How easily assets may be converted into cash without substantially affecting the asset's price.

Load Fees: A sales charge assessed by some mutual funds. The fee is paid by the investor and is passed along as compensation to the salesperson. If assessed on a purchase of a mutual fund, it is referred to as an up-front or front-end load. Sales charges assessed at the time of a sale are referred to as back-end loads. Many mutual funds do not have load fees, and those funds are referred to as no-load mutual funds.

Market Risk: The possibility of loss an investor faces due to factors that affect the overall performance of the financial markets. Market risk cannot be eliminated with diversification. Often called Systemic Risk, market risk arises because of uncertainties in the economy, political environment, natural or human-made disasters, or recession.

Market Value: Current market price of a security as indicated by the last trade recorded.

Maturity: The date on which a debt is payable or due.

Minimum Hold Time: To discourage short-term trading, a mutual fund may assess a load or fee upon sale if the mutual fund is not held long enough. The minimum hold time generally ranges from ninety days to one year.

Money Market (Deposit) Account: An interest-bearing account at a bank or credit union.

Money Market Mutual Fund: A kind of mutual fund that invests in highly liquid, short-term debt securities, cash, and cash equivalents with a goal to maintain a stable asset value and provide income.

Mortgage-Backed Securities: An investment secured by a mortgage or group of mortgages purchased from the entities that issued the mortgages. They are a type of asset-backed security.

Municipal Bond: A debt obligation issued by a state or local government or territory or one of their agencies. Funds raised by a municipal bond issue are generally used to finance public projects such as roads, schools, airports, or infrastructure repairs.

Mutual Fund: An investment product that pools money from many investors to purchase securities such as stocks, bonds, and money market instruments. Mutual funds give small or individual investors access to diversified professionally managed portfolios.

National Credit Union Share Insurance Fund (NCUSIF): The NCUSIF provides deposit insurance to protect the accounts of credit union members at federally insured institutions in the United States.

Net Asset Value (NAV): The value of a mutual fund's assets minus the value of its liabilities. When divided by the number of outstanding shares, it represents a mutual fund's per share market value.

Open-End Mutual Funds: Mutual funds that issue and redeem shares on a continuous basis so that they grow or shrink in response to investor demand for shares.

Operating Expense Ratio (OER): A measure of a mutual fund's or ETF's operating cost relative to its assets. An expense ratio of 1% per annum means that each year, 1% of the fund's total assets will be used to cover expenses. The expense ratio does not include sales loads or brokerage commissions.

Orders (Trading): Instruction to a broker or dealer to buy or sell a security.

Over-the-Counter Market: A decentralized market in which securities are traded directly between two parties without a central exchange.

Ownership Category/Capacity: Description used by the FDIC/ SIPC to define depositors qualifying for separate insurance coverage.

Par Value: See **Face Value**.

Passive Management: A style of portfolio management associated with mutual funds and ETFs that mirrors or replicates a market index.

Portfolio: A range of investments held by a person or organization.

Premium: An amount by which a CD or bond trades above its face (par) value.

Principal: The original sum invested or lent.

Prospectus: A formal written offer issued by a mutual fund that describes the history, background of managers, fund objectives, financial statement, and other data. Other types of offerings may also require a prospectus: a school, commercial enterprise, or book, for example.

Purchasing Power: The value of money as measured by the goods and services it can buy. Inflation decreases that amount of goods and services.

Rate of Interest: The rate paid to savers for keeping money in an account, or the rate lenders charge to borrow money. It is usually expressed as a percentage.

Real Estate Investment Trust (REIT): A company that owns, and in most cases, operates, income-producing real estate.

Rebalance: The action to bring a portfolio that has deviated from its target asset allocation back into line.

Redemption Fee: A charge by a mutual fund company to discourage a purchase followed by a sale within a short period of time. Also called a short-term trading fee.

Registered Investment Advisor (RIA): A firm registered with the SEC or a state's securities agency to give investment advice about securities to clients. They may also manage investment portfolios. **An RIA must act as a fiduciary.** The firm is called an RIA while its employees are called Investment Advisor Representatives (IARs).

Registration: Legal description of the ownership of an account.

Risk Capacity: Risk capacity is the amount of risk an organization or individual requires to meet their goals. Risk capacity is commonly compared to risk tolerance, or the willingness to take on risk.

Risk Profile/Risk Tolerance: The degree of variability in investment returns that an investor is willing to withstand.

Risk Tolerance Questionnaire: A set of questions that help identify an investor's attitude toward investing, their understanding of financial markets, and how they may react during certain investment market and economic conditions.

Robo-Advisor: Digital financial advice based on mathematical rules or algorithms, which are executed by software. The software utilizes its algorithms to automatically allocate, manage, and optimize clients' assets.

S&P 500 Index: A stock market index that measures the stock performance of 500 large companies listed on stock exchanges in the United States.

Sales Charge: A fee paid as compensation to a salesperson by a buyer of shares in a load mutual fund. See **Load Fees**.

Saving: The process of setting aside a portion of current income for future use.

Savings Account: An account at a bank, credit union, or saving institution that earns interest. There may be restrictions, such as the number of withdrawals. The provider of a savings account sometimes offers an ATM card.

Savings and Loan/Mutual Savings Bank: A type of state or federally chartered financial institution that focuses on accepting savings deposits and making residential mortgages and other consumer loans. Savings and loans can be organized like a bank (owned by investor shareholders) or a credit union (owned by the depositors).

Sector: A subset of the economy in which businesses share the same or a related product or service.

Securities: Tradable financial assets that hold some type of monetary value. They can represent an ownership interest such as stock; a creditor relationship such as bonds; or rights to ownership such as options.

Securities Investor Protection Corporation (SIPC): A nonprofit corporation created to insure the securities and cash in investor accounts of member brokerage firms against failure of those firms.

Share: Units of equity ownership of a company, limited partnership, ETF, or mutual fund.

Short-Term Trading Fee: A charge by a mutual fund company to discourage a purchase followed by a sale within a short period of time. Also called a redemption fee.

Sovereign Debt: Debt issued by a central government.

Stock Dividend: A sum of money paid by a company to its shareholders out of its profits or reserves.

Stock Exchange: An organized marketplace where stockbrokers and traders can buy and sell securities such as stock, ETFs, and some bonds. The security must be listed on the exchange and brokers and dealers must be members of the exchange to be able to trade.

Stockholder/Shareholder: The holder of shares of stock, which represent ownership of a company. Mutual fund owners are also called shareholders.

Systemic Risk: The possibility of loss an investor faces due to factors that affect the overall performance of the financial markets. Systemic risk cannot be eliminated with diversification. Often called Market Risk, it arises because of uncertainties in the economy, political environment, natural or human-made disasters, or recession.

Target Date Mutual Fund: A type of asset allocation fund that starts with a higher risk investment mix but moves toward lower risk as the investor approaches some predetermined date. Other names for this type of mutual fund are Lifecycle Funds or Age-Based Funds.

Tax-Advantaged Account: A type of financial account or savings plan that is either exempt from taxation, taxes are deferred, or that offers other types of tax benefits.

Taxable Account: A type of financial account in which taxes on income—interest, dividends, and capital gains—must be paid each year.

Thrift Institution: See **Savings and Loan/Mutual Savings Bank**

Time Horizon: The period one expects to hold an investment until all, or part of the money is needed.

Time the Market: A strategy of making decisions to buy or sell a financial asset by attempting to predict future market price movements.

Trade Date: The day on which you buy or sell a security. The settlement date, on which cash or securities are delivered, usually comes one or more days later.

Trading Symbol: A unique series of letters (and sometimes numbers) assigned to a security for trading purposes.

Trust Account: A legal arrangement through which funds or assets are held by a third party (the trustee) for the benefit of another party (the beneficiary). The creator of the trust is known as a grantor or settlor.

U.S. Securities and Exchange Commission (SEC): An independent agency of the United States federal government. It holds primary responsibility for enforcing the federal securities laws, proposing rules, and regulating the securities industry.

Variable Discretionary Expenses: Expenses that can change over time, for example, month to month. Some variable costs represent necessities like groceries and gas for a car. Some represent non-necessities or discretionary items like restaurants, golf, or movies.

Volatility: A measurement of how much and how often the price of an investment moves up and down over time. Volatility is also used to talk about market or investment portfolio behavior. It is a measure of risk.

Volatility Risk: The risk of price swings not in your favor.

Weighted Average: A calculation of return that considers the degrees of importance of the numbers in the set. Each number is multiplied by its weight (importance) before the average is calculated.

Yield: The return to an investor. A bond's yield is derived from the cash flows of the interest payments and its maturity payment.

SOURCES:

Barron's Dictionary of Finance and Investment Terms
Investopedia